THE
GOOD
CAKE
BOOK

THE GOOD CAKE BOOK

by
Diana Dalsass

Illustrated with linecuts by
Lloyd Birmingham

NAL BOOKS
NEW AMERICAN LIBRARY
TIMES MIRROR
NEW YORK AND SCARBOROUGH, ONTARIO

Again, to my husband, Mario—my biggest fan and severest taster—who could not get through the day without at least one piece of homemade cake.

NAL BOOKS TRADEMARK REG. U.S. PAT. OFF. AND FOREIGN COUNTRIES
REGISTERED TRADEMARK—MARCA REGISTRADA
HECHO EN CRAWFORDSVILLE, INDIANA, U.S.A.

SIGNET, SIGNET CLASSICS, MENTOR, PLUME, MERIDIAN AND
NAL BOOKS are published in the United States by
The New American Library, Inc.,
1633 Broadway, New York, New York 10019,
in Canada by The New American Library of Canada Limited,
81 Mack Avenue, Scarborough, Ontario M1L 1M8

Library of Congress Cataloging in Publication Data

Dalsass, Diana.
The good cake book.

Includes index.
1. Cake.   I. Title.
TX771.D34   1982   641.8′653   82-12621
ISBN 0-453-00432-6

Designed by Leonard Telesca

First Printing, November, 1982

1 2 3 4 5 6 7 8 9

PRINTED IN THE UNITED STATES OF AMERICA

Contents

BAR CAKES   151

A SELECTION OF BASIC ICINGS . . . For Those Who Won't Eat Cake Without Them   231

Introduction

This is a book for cake lovers, for people who, like myself, experience supreme pleasure when biting into a well-made, densely-textured piece of cake. I do want to establish one thing straight off, though—if you're one of those who eat cake only to get at the icing, this book isn't for you. Rather, these are cakes that, in themselves, are so flavorful and marvelously satisfying, they stand alone (although I have included a few icing recipes for those who just won't eat cake without it). Here, gathered into a single volume, are everyone's best-loved cakes—carrot filled with crunchy walnuts, sinfully dark chocolate, tender banana, moist applesauce, tangy cranberry, spicy gingerbread, and on and on—what I like to think of as "good" cakes.

What's more, every recipe in this book can be whipped up in 30 minutes or less (plus time for baking, of course). And because these cakes need no icing, most can be sampled warm from the oven. What more could you ask of a dessert than instant gratification?

As any cake lover knows, an almost endless number of occasions present themselves for enjoying these quickly prepared treats. While sweeter, more elaborate-looking layer cakes are generally reserved for special parties, these homey cakes make ideal mid-morning or afternoon snacks, wrap well for lunch-box goodies, and are also fine family desserts. Coffee cakes and "quick" breads (really a type of loaf cake) make any breakfast or brunch more festive. And if you're entertaining, a scoop of ice cream or dollop of whipped cream takes almost any of these cakes into the realm of party fare. As an additional bonus, while you'd never slice into a layer cake before serving it to guests, no one need ever know that you've enjoyed a preliminary nibble of one of these if you simply cut the cake into squares or slices and arrange them on a pretty platter.

THE BASICS OF CAKE BAKING

One reason why cake baking is so quick and easy (and nearly fool-proof, incidentally) is that there are only two basic methods for combining the ingredients; and all the recipes in this book fall into one of these two categories.

Method for Butter Cakes

By far, the most common type of cake is the (solid) butter cake (I will discuss the use of butter versus margarine later). The procedure is always identical; all that varies is the choice of flavorings for the individual cake. Here's a rundown of the steps involved:

1. The butter is first creamed with the sugar (or molasses or honey). For best results, the butter should be quite soft, but not melting or oily, before beginning. Mix the sugar into the butter until the butter is very light and fluffy, with the sugar completely incorporated into it. While you may use a heavy spoon for this step, an electric mixer does a far quicker job that's easier on your arm muscles, as well. (At the end of this section, I will discuss how to prepare cake batters using a food processor.)

2. Next, the eggs (or just the yolks if the whites are to be beaten separately) are beaten into the butter-sugar mixture. These should also be beaten very well, until the mixture looks completely uniform. Many recipes instruct the cook to beat in the eggs one at a time. I have always found this to be a great bother and totally unnecessary, so long as they are thoroughly beaten before proceeding to the next step.

3. Now the liquid ingredients and flavorings, such as milk, juice, applesauce, vanilla extract, pumpkin puree, etc., are beaten into the batter. The consistency will now be quite liquid and may even look curdled, but this is fine. Some recipes instruct the baker to add the liquid ingredients alternately with the dry ones, but here's another example of an unnecessary, bothersome, and time-consuming procedure.

4. The dry ingredients—flour, leavening, salt, and spices—are now stirred together in a separate bowl. With today's light flours, it is not necessary to sift the dry ingredients or to sift the flour before measuring it. This simply creates extra utensils for you to wash and adds to the preparation time. There are, however, three exceptions to this general rule: (a) If your flour has become lumpy, you will certainly want to sift it; (b) If you are adding cocoa, which has a great tendency to form hard pellets in the tin, it may be necessary to sift it; and (c) If you are making a very delicate torte or angel food cake, sifting the flour may produce a better-textured result.

5. The dry ingredients are then beaten or stirred into the liquid ones. You must be careful not to overbeat; mix only until the flour is fully incorporated.

6. Occasionally a recipe will call for the egg whites to be beaten separately. As this takes longer and uses an extra bowl, most of my recipes don't require this step. But on those occasions when a cake does benefit from added lightness due to beaten egg whites, I certainly take the trouble to do it, in which case they would be folded in gently, but thoroughly at this point.

7. Finally, any hard ingredients, such as fresh or dried fruits, nuts, or chocolate chips, are stirred into the batter.

8. As the last step, the batter is turned into a greased and floured pan and baked in a preheated oven. Be certain that your oven temperature gauge is accurate; a fault here affects cakes far more adversely than it would vegetables or casseroles.

A cake is done when a toothpick inserted in the center comes out clean. Additional signs of doneness are if the edges have pulled away slightly from the sides of the pan and if the cake feels springy when you touch it. Let the cake cool on a rack, and don't remove it from the pan until it has cooled to room temperature (although you can cut yourself a piece from the pan for immediate enjoyment).

Food Processor Method for Butter Cakes

If you own a food processor, the steps in preparing a cake batter are all identical to those described above, only speeded up immeasurably. Here are some tips:

- Always use the steel blade.
- If the cake is small (an 8" x 8" or 9" x 9" square pan or a 9" x 5" loaf pan), the entire batter can be prepared in your work bowl. If the cake is larger (a layer cake, tube cake, or 9" x 13" oblong), process everything except the dry ingredients in the work bowl. Then, by hand, mix the contents of the work bowl with the dry ingredients in a large mixing bowl.
- If the recipe calls for lemon or orange rind, you need not grate it separately. Simply peel the citrus fruit with a vegetable peeler and add the rind to the work bowl in step 1 with the butter and sugar. By the time the sugar has been incorporated into the butter, the peel will be finely shredded.
- Ingredients to be chopped, such as nuts, cranberries, apples, chocolate, etc., can either be processed before you start making the batter, removed from the work bowl, and stirred in after the dry ingredients have been added, or, for a small cake, added to the work bowl after the last of the liquid ingredients has been processed into the batter—simply add the nuts or whatever and process until they are chopped to the desired size.

Method for Oil (or Melted Butter) Cakes

Tortes, brownies, chiffon cakes, and carrot cakes are among those that most commonly fit into this category. For the most part, the procedure is very similar to that described for (solid) butter cakes. It is only in the first two steps that the directions differ:

1. The eggs are beaten quite well (with an electric mixer or food processor). Then the sugar is added very gradually, beating all the while. When finished, the mixture should be very thick and pale yellow in color. It is this thorough beating that gives cakes of this type their characteristic pleasant, slightly chewy texture.

2. The oil or slightly cooled, melted butter is beaten into the egg mixture. From this point, the procedure is the same as for butter cakes.

Ingredients

SHORTENING

There is no question but that butter has a finer, fresher flavor than margarine. But butter is considerably more expensive. Butter is also high in saturated fats, which the majority of nutritionists in this country feel can contribute to heart and other disorders.

However, margarine is not a perfect food, either. Most brands contain a handful of additives that serve as preservatives, flavorings, and color enhancers. And the question as to which additives are entirely safe for human consumption is yet to be resolved. Also, not all margarines contain the same proportions of unsaturated fats to saturated. This information is generally displayed on the box; a ratio of 2:1 (unsaturated to saturated) will usually insure a more healthful product than one with more (or even *all*) saturated fats. As a final caveat, when the polyunsaturated liquid oils that go into margarine are processed to make them solid, the chemical structure changes, and the resulting fat may be quite different from anything nature produces on its own.

Despite the possible problems associated with margarine, I usually use it in cakes for reasons of both health and economy. However, certain cakes, such as pound cakes or other buttery-flavored cakes, really do need real butter to taste best. In most recipes, I specify butter or margarine, and you may make the choice yourself. But when the flavor of butter is essential, I state this, and you really should try to use at least half butter.

Some cakes call for a liquid shortening, usually oil. I have found, however, that oil can produce an unpleasant, slightly oily texture. In recipes of this type, I use melted margarine, which generally produces a better result.

SUGAR

Most cakes call for plain granulated sugar. Refined white sugar has come into a great deal of disrepute during the last several years because it supplies "empty calories"—that is, calories with no accompanying nutritional value. However, what many people don't realize is that honey is nearly as devoid of nutrition as sugar. You'd have to consume a whole pound of honey to get approximately the same quantity of vitamins and minerals as in a single serving of many vegetables. What's more, honey is far more expensive than sugar.

The fact is that no sweetener—white sugar, brown sugar, honey, or even molasses with its high mineral content—is particularly good for you when consumed in excess. But eaten in moderation, as in the amount in a single piece of cake, there is no harm to your body unless you are a diabetic. The simple sugar present in refined white sugar has the same chemical structure as that contained in fresh and dried fruits, foods considered to be healthful. And once the sugar enters your body, it doesn't matter what food source it came from.

Cake should be regarded as the "treat" that it is. Eat a variety of foods to make up a complete diet, and indulge in cake as often as your waistline permits. But please do not imagine that interchanging honey for the sugar will magically make the cake any better for you.

Because white sugar is an economical, all-purpose sweetener, the majority of recipes in this book call for it as an ingredient. Occasionally, of course, the distinctive flavor of brown sugar, honey, or molasses is more appropriate to a particular cake. These cakes aren't any better tasting or any better for you; they are simply equally delicious in their own right.

LIQUIDS

The most common liquid used in cake batters is milk or a milk product such as yogurt or sour cream.

When milk is specified in a recipe, you may use whole, low-fat, skimmed, or reconstituted nonfat dry milk. The slightly different fat content of each will not affect the final result.

When "sour" milk or buttermilk is specified, you may make your own substitute from sweet milk. For each cup called for, place a tablespoon of vinegar or lemon juice in the bottom of the cup, fill it to the 1-cup mark with milk, and stir. You may also use plain yogurt as a substitute. Do not use milk that has gone bad or sour in the refrigerator due to age, as it may not be healthful.

When yogurt is specified, you may substitute buttermilk or "sour" milk, made as directed above.

And finally, when sour cream is called for in a recipe, there is no other ingredient that can exactly duplicate the marvelous texture and flavor this lends to a cake. However, if there is a recipe you are anxious to make on the spur of the moment and you're out of sour cream, you can substitute yogurt, buttermilk, or "sour" milk and add an extra tablespoon of butter for each cup of sour cream called for.

Other liquids commonly used in cake batters include water, alcohol, fruit juices, and fruit and vegetable purées. These are quite self-explanatory, and any necessary extra notes are included in the particular recipe.

FLOUR

Whenever I specify flour in this book, I am referring to all-purpose white flour, which may be bleached or unbleached as you prefer. Except in a very few instances, it is not necessary to use cake flour in recipes. Cake flour is finer and produces a very light texture which, to my mind, is not compatible with the hearty cakes featured in this book.

You may be surprised to find whole wheat flour called for in several recipes throughout the book. This type of flour, which is produced by milling the wheat germ and bran along with the starchy grain, is heartier and more flavorful, not to mention more nutritious than white flour. Whole wheat flour is particularly appealing in such cakes as carrot, spice, and banana. Because this type of flour is heavier than white, I usually use half of each to achieve the advantages of both.

ROLLED OATS

Rolled oats may be purchased in three forms—old-fashioned, quick-cooking, and instant. Old-fashioned and quick-cooking rolled oats are identical except that for old-fashioned rolled oats the oat groat is left intact, while the groat for quick-cooking oats is cut into several pieces before rolling.

Either old-fashioned or quick-cooking oats may be used in the recipes in this book. I prefer the quick-cooking form because it produces a slightly lighter textured cake. Old-fashioned oats make for more body and greater chewiness.

Instant oats have been highly processed, and their powderiness will affect the characteristic oatmeal texture we so enjoy. Instant oats are also considerably more expensive than the old-fashioned or quick-cooking varieties.

Note: Unless a recipe specifies cooked oatmeal, all rolled oat measurements are for the *raw* rolled oats, measured directly from the box.

CHOCOLATE

When chocolate flavors the entire cake batter (as opposed to bits of sweet or semisweet chocolate scattered throughout the batter), generally unsweetened chocolate is used. This may be in the form of chocolate squares or cocoa. Both produce similar results, when the proper conversion for fat content is followed, though perhaps the chocolate squares are somewhat richer and more flavorful.

If a recipe calls for unsweetened chocolate and you only have cocoa in the kitchen, for each 1-ounce square of chocolate, you may substitute 3 tablespoons of unsweetened cocoa powder plus 1 tablespoon of butter. (Do not use cocoa mixes that contain milk and/or sugar.) Likewise, if a recipe specifies cocoa, you may use one 1-ounce square of chocolate minus 1 tablespoon of butter for every 3 tablespoons of cocoa.

Just a note on melting chocolate: Because chocolate melts (and burns) at a low temperature, it's easy to scorch it if you're not careful. Many cookbooks suggest melting chocolate in a double boiler. Although this eliminates the risk of burning the chocolate, it does take longer. I've always found this precaution unnecessary, so long as you're careful to use a very low heat, to stir the chocolate occasionally, and to remove the pot from the heat as soon as the chocolate has melted.

VANILLA

Since so many people vacation in Mexico these days, I must tell you that Mexican vanilla is far superior to the domestic product. I have seen it for sale there in markets, as well as in gift shops. The taste is so deliciously subtle that our own vanilla extract seems almost chemical by contrast. If you are not planning a trip to Mexico, it may be possible to purchase a bottle in a Mexican or Spanish market of a city with a large Hispanic population.

If you must resort to domestic vanilla, please use only the pure extract. Artificial vanilla flavor tastes just that—artificial.

Some General Notes on Baking

MEASURING CUPS

An enormous amount of time can be saved by using the graduated measuring cups that come in ¼-cup, ⅓-cup, ½-cup, and 1-cup sizes. For measuring flour, sugar, or any other dry ingredient, all you need do is scoop the cup into the bag or canister, filling it to overflowing, and level it off with a knife. A cup of flour measured this way requires about 5 seconds;

it takes far longer to fill a glass cup, a spoonful at a time, while constantly leveling off the flour to see if the correct marker has yet been reached.

For measuring liquids, although you can use the dry measuring cups, it's probably easier to use the glass ones because liquids have a tendency to spill over when the cup is filled to the top.

PREPARATION OF BAKING PANS

You will encounter no problems in removing cakes from their baking pans if you grease and flour them before spooning in the batter. Simply smear all inside surfaces with shortening or margarine (butter is rather an extravagance here). Then sprinkle about a tablespoon of flour in the pan and tilt the pan to spread the flour to all surfaces. Turn the pan upside down and rap it with your fist a couple of times to dislodge any extra flour.

When the cake comes from the oven, run a knife around the edges. After the cake has cooled to room temperature, again run a knife around the edges, this time pulling up gently on the bottom to dislodge it from the pan. When you have gone around the whole rim, you should be able to simply tip the cake upside down over a plate and have it easily slide out. If you are baking a tube cake (which is somewhat more fragile than a flat cake), you will find that it is easier to remove the cake from the pan if the central cone and bottom of the pan form a separate piece from the outer rim. Then you can remove the whole cake from the outer rim and run a knife along the bottom before removing it from the pan.

BAKING PAN SIZES

If you bake cakes often, you probably own baking pans in several different sizes. But even if your kitchen is equipped with only a few pans, many sizes are interchangeable. For flat cakes (those baked in square, round, or oblong pans), just compute the number of square inches in the pan specified in a recipe and then use the pan you own with the closest size to this. If the cake is a little flatter or higher, the final result will still be fine. Just add or subtract a few minutes from the baking time to compensate for the different thickness.

For example, if a recipe specifies a 9" x 9" square pan (81 square inches), you can substitute an 8" x 10" oblong pan (80 square inches). You may find that the baking time will be increased by 5 minutes. Likewise, if a recipe specifies a 9" x 13" oblong pan (117 square inches), you could substitute two 9" round layer cake pans (61 square inches each = 122 square inches total). Test the cake for doneness about 10 minutes before the time specified in the recipe.

When a tube cake pan is called for, you may use a 9" or 10" flat-bottomed tube pan or a scalloped bundt pan of similar size. If you prefer, the cake could also be baked in two 9" x 5" loaf pans. Begin testing the loaves about 10 minutes before the time specified in the recipe.

A cake batter that calls for a tube or loaf pan may or may not bake properly in a flat pan (and vice versa). If you really wish to convert from one to the other, all you can do is try it out and hope for the best.

STORAGE OF CAKES

It is much easier to properly store an unfrosted cake than one with gooey icing that sticks to plastic wrap, a cream-filled cake that readily spoils, or a quick-to-sog meringue-topped cake.

Plain cakes of the type in this book simply must be protected from drying out. You may cover them with plastic wrap or foil, or place them in one of those plastic cake-keepers. Most of the cakes in this book will stay fresh for at least a week if properly wrapped.

For longer storage, the cakes may be frozen. When I make a large tube cake, I often freeze a big chunk of it right away. Then, several weeks later, when I again have a yen for this cake, it's right there in the freezer. Frozen cakes, either whole or in nice-sized pieces, are also marvelous to have on hand when unexpected guests drop by. Cakes thaw very quickly at room temperature. Keep them wrapped while thawing so they don't dry out.

Depending on the moistness of the cake and also the temperature and humidity of your home, you may wish to refrigerate the cake as well as wrap it. The plainer cakes, such as gingerbread, brownies, banana loaves, and "quick" breads, generally fare fine at room temperature unless it's a humid mid-summer's day. However, most of the cakes that contain fresh fruits are very moist and should be refrigerated, particularly during the warm months, as a protection against spoilage. If you prefer to eat your cake at room temperature, just remove it from the refrigerator an hour or so before dessert.

THE CAKES

That covers the basics of cake baking. Just a few simple steps, and you have a host of marvelous, impressive cakes in your repertoire. Now that your mouth is watering, let's get on to the recipes themselves.

The recipes are organized into eight sections roughly according to ingredients, with such broad headings as "Cakes with Fruits," "Cakes with Vegetables," and so on, plus a final section of icing recipes. Of course, there's much overlap, since many recipes contain ingredients that fit into more than one section. I have provided an index in the back of the book, so that if you're craving a chocolate cake, for example, you'll easily be able to find all the chocolate cake recipes in the book. The hard part will be deciding which one to make!

Cakes fit into other categories as well, for instance, the occasions for which they are made. Some we view as special-occasion desserts, others are ideal for brunch, while still others have a homeyness that makes them cold-weather treats. Below, I have listed some of the cake recipes in this book in various different occasion categories. Just use this listing as a suggested guide, though. There's no reason why "Gift Cakes" shouldn't be enjoyed by you, or a slice of a "Special Occasion Cake" used as a lunch-box treat.

Hearty Fall and Winter Dessert Cakes

There are more cakes that fit into this category than any other, probably because it is my favorite type—and a lot of other people's too. Although these cakes are delicious during the cold months and contain ingredients available year-round, there's no reason to wait until the frost is on the ground to enjoy such emminently satisfying desserts.

Fresh Apple Spice Cake
Applesauce–Cranberry Sauce Cake
Applesauce Raisin Bran Cake
Gingered Banana Cake
Cranberry Molasses Cake
Lemon Cake
Fresh Fruit Fruitcake
Classic Pineapple Upside-Down Cake
Pear Cake
New England Carrot Cake
Old-Fashioned Glazed Pineapple–Carrot Cake
Fresh Yam Cake
Chocolate Cherry Ring
Potato Fudge Cake
Bittersweet Chocolate Marble Cake
Double Chocolate Cake
Butterscotch Chocolate Chip Cake
Old-Fashioned Gingerbread
Glazed Prune Spice Cake
Extra-Moist Chocolate Banana Bars
Peanut Butter Fruit Bars
Marmorkuchen (German Marble Cake)
Graham Sour Cream Cake
Bran Streusel Cake

Light Spring and Summer Dessert Cakes

Most of these cakes make use of seasonal ingredients. I often wonder, if fresh peaches were available year-round, would they still evoke such strong images of lazy, sun-warmed days?

Because these cakes can only be baked when the fruits are at their peak, if you miss the Peach-Filled Cake, for example, this summer, it will be another year before you again have the chance to savor it.

A few other recipes were placed in this list because they are so light, they make perfect accompaniments to ice cream or the fresh fruits of summer.

Blueberry Whipped Cream Cake
Souffléed Lemon Cake
Peach Graham Upside-Down Torte
Peach-Filled Cake
Grape Cupcakes
Springtime Rhubarb Cake
Santa Rosa Plum Cake
Yugoslavian Chocolate Cake
Fresh Strawberry Bread
Sponge Cake

Special-Occasion Cakes

These are party cakes—sensational to look at, a little more expensive to prepare, and festive enough to please your guests. What's especially delightful about these cakes is that they, like all the other cakes in this book, can be made in advance. Unlike so many other company desserts, a superlative cake requires no last-minute fussing or time away from your guests.

A word of warning, though! Once you glance at these recipes, you'll either be forced to throw a party immediately—or just break down and try a few for yourself. They are *that* irresistible!

Tropical Banana Cake
Orange Pecan Cake
Chocolate Zucchini Cake
Richest-*Ever* Chocolate Pound Cake
Mississippi Mud Cake
Double Chocolate Marble Cake
Chocolate Almond Pound Cake

Chocolate Chip Apple Cake
Spiced Honey Chiffon Cake
Gingered Vodka Cake
Poppy Seed Cake
Polish Chocolate Almond Bars
Almond Rum Cake
Raspberry Nut Butter Cake
Austrian Nut Cake
Hazelnut Cake
Piña Colada Cake

Holiday Cakes

Festive cakes enliven any Thanksgiving or Christmas table and are perfect to have on hand when guests drop by during the holiday season. Pumpkin and mincemeat cakes are unusual alternatives to the customary pies, and the Chocolate "Plum Pudding" Cake requires far less work than a traditional steamed pudding. All of these recipes are easy enough for every day, but fancy enough for those special days.

Upside-Down Cranberry Gingerbread
Festive Pumpkin Cake
Pumpkin Chocolate Chip Cake
Chocolate "Plum Pudding" Cake
German Christmas Gingerbread
Holiday Fruit and Nut Spice Cake
Cranberry Sauce Loaf
Spiced Pumpkin Loaf
Stollen
Mincemeat Upside-Down Cake
French Fruitcake

Gift Cakes

Particularly during the holiday season, a loaf of cranberry bread, a spice cake, or a batch of brownies makes a great gift when you're visiting friends or relatives. Those listed below all have the advantage of transporting well. Wrap them in foil and hand-carry; or cushion them with tissue paper and mail as a personal way of expressing holiday greetings to someone far away.

Applesauce Oatmeal Cake
Cranberry Rum-Raisin Bars
Mincemeat Spice Cake
Brownies, or one of the variations
Cranberry Chocolate Bars
German Christmas Bars
Raisin Nut Spice Bars
Cranberry-Orange Bread
Lemon Bread
Pineapple–Zucchini Loaf

Children's Cakes

Children are notoriously picky when it comes to food. In my own experience, I've found that children don't like things with strange colors, unfamiliar ingredients, strong spices, or textures that are too hard or too soft. The cakes listed below contain some of children's most beloved ingredients—chocolate, bananas, peanut butter, applesauce, etc. Of course, all children have their own additional dislikes—if your youngster "hates" peanut butter, don't expect the Peanut Butter Raisin Bread to be a winner. In general, though, children love cakes—and these recipes in particular will appeal to most tots.

Incidentally, don't limit these cakes to children. Adults, too, find these ingredients immensely satisfying. I have yet to meet anyone at *any* age who didn't flip over my Chocolate Chip Cake.

Peanut Butter Applesauce Cake
Banana Chocolate Chip Cake
Orange Oatmeal Cake
California Fudge Cake
Chocolate Banana Cake
Chocolate Maraschino Cake

Chocolate Peanut Butter Cake
Chocolate Syrup Cake
Fudge Chip Cake
Chocolate Crunch-Topped Cake
Chocolate Chip Cake
Milk Chocolate Oatmeal Bars
Peanut Banana Bars
Pumpkin Molasses Bread
Peanut Butter Raisin Bread

BRUNCH AND MORNING COFFEE CAKES

Coffee cakes and "quick" breads are ideal for weekend brunches or as an accompaniment to a cup of mid-morning coffee, either enjoyed alone or when a friend drops by. These cakes are not too sweet or rich and so seem appropriate for the morning hours. If you're planning a brunch that requires last-minute cooking (scrambled eggs, sausages, etc.), you'll really appreciate having one component of the meal that can be made in advance. And a homemade coffee cake, besides being easy on you, is one of those always-popular foods that will win accolades from your guests.

Apple Sour Cream Streusel Cake
Banana Oatmeal Crumb Cake
Blueberry Cream Cheese Cake
Blueberry Banana Bread
Pumpkin Wheat Ring
Grandmother's Date and Nut Bread
Crunch-Topped Coffee Cake
Pecan Swirl Cake
Black Forest Coffee Cake

Between-Meal Snack Cakes

These cakes are even less sweet than coffee cakes and are perfect for times when you want a little something with a cup of coffee or tea but aren't in the mood for a real dessert. Many of these recipes are from European countries, where desserts are either whipped-cream-filled tortes served on special occasions or very simple cakes and cookies enjoyed daily. Cakes like the Tyrolean Nut Cake, Almond Biscotti, or British Tea Loaf are appropriate at all hours and are especially pleasing as late-night snacks.

Orange Almond Tea Loaf
Candied Orange Loaf
Lemon Loaf
German Anise Cake
British Caraway Cake
Toasted Sesame Cake
Banana Nut Bread
Fresh Rhubarb Bread
Apple–Carrot Bread
British Tea Loaf
Graham Cracker Bread
Almond Biscotti
Tyrolean Nut Cake
Cognac French Cakes
Lemon-Filled Macaroon

Lunch-Box Cakes

These goodies are easy to wrap, easy to pack, and are conveniently sliced or cut into squares for individual servings. They're hearty, not terribly sweet, and keep well. Adults and children alike would welcome any of these in their lunch boxes. Keep these recipes in mind, too, when you're planning a picnic.

Cranberry–Orange Cupcakes
Simple Carrot Loaf
Chocolate Applesauce Cake
Jam Cake
Chocolate Cream Cheese Bars
Walnut Fudge Bars
Mocha-Crunch Yogurt Bars

Honey Bran Jam Bars
Spiced Squash Bars
Health Bars
Banana–Carrot Bread
Carrot–Zucchini Bread
Grape Nut Bread
Honey Sunflower Cake
Vermont Wine Loaf

Warm-from-the-Oven Cakes

While none of the cakes in this book requires icing and most can be eaten right from the oven, some cakes (such as those baked in tube or loaf pans) are really better if allowed to cool to room temperature before enjoying. But the cakes listed below *taste best* when they still have that warm, just-baked flavor. These cakes are perfect when you're in the mood for a piece of cake *right now*. Because they're all baked in square or oblong pans, the baking times are short. So in many instances, it's less than an hour between that first yearning and the ready-to-eat cake.

Applesauce Molasses Cake
Banana Crumb Cake
Cranberry Oatmeal Cobbler-Cake
Orange Juice Cake
Pumpkin–Prune Cake
Honeyed Chocolate Upside-Down Cake
Chocolate Molasses Cake
Mocha Nut Devil's Food Cake
Chunky Cake
Vermont Gingerbread
English Crumb Cake
Banana Molasses Bars
Grape Nut Cake

Cakes With Fruits

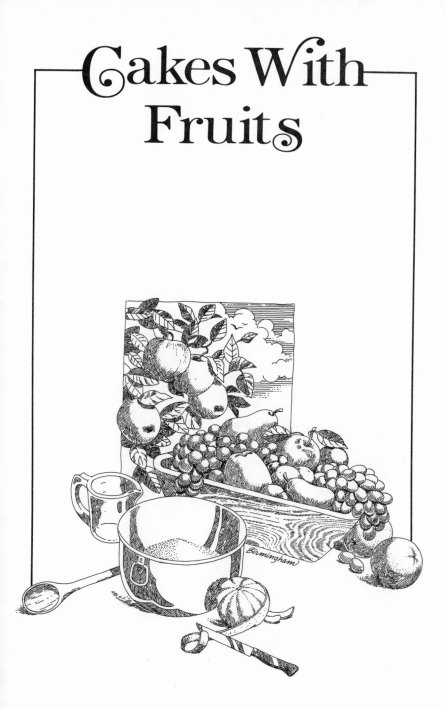

I think I could write a book devoted just to cakes containing fresh fruits. As each season of the year arrives, bringing with it its own marvelous variety of fruits, I dig out all the recipes I have been holding in wait for these ingredients to again be available.

Thus, the end of summer finds me making lovely cakes with sensually dark Italian prune plums, fall has me buying bags of tart, brilliantly red cranberries, and as summer arrives, I rush to bake homey cakes filled with tender ripe peaches and beautiful tangy blueberries. Apples, one of the most ideal of fruits for cakes, fortunately can be purchased nearly year-round.

In almost all instances, it is far preferable to use fresh fruits over the canned or frozen ones. Perhaps one exception is pineapple—canned pineapple, especially when packed in juice, is quite delectable in cakes and certainly saves on the tedious work of preparing the fresh fruit. But there is really no adequate substitute for fresh apples, peaches, blueberries, or cranberries. When a recipe calls for applesauce, however, the store-bought variety is convenient and acceptable enough; because it is generally somewhat more watery than home-made applesauce, though, the apple flavor will be less intense.

When you're making a cake from this chapter of the book, have the fruit ready for the batter before you begin. Many fruits require almost no preparation: Bananas need only be peeled and mashed; blueberries and cranberries are just washed and picked over; and plums are halved and pitted. Peaches, if they are to be peeled, take a bit longer, only because they are so juicy. Apples require the longest preparation time. But fortunately, you need far fewer apples for cake batters than for pies or applesauce, so even this step goes quite quickly. And all that peeling, coring, and chopping is certainly worth it when you get to bite into that fragrant, fresh apple cake.

Cakes With Fresh Apples

Some varieties of apple are known for their crisp texture and tart flavor, while others are preferred for their sweetness. What type of apple you choose for cakes is really a matter of preference . . . and availability. Myself, I like the decided tangy crispness of Winesaps and buy them whenever I can. However, the sweeter McIntosh and Red and Golden Delicious apples are most prevalent in the supermarkets throughout the year. Or, if you wish to splurge a bit, Granny Smith apples are excellent for both cooking and eating.

HONEYED APPLE CAKE

Lots of fresh apple chunks team up with honey, coffee, and grated lemon rind to flavor this hearty tube cake.

⅔ cup (10⅔ tablespoons) butter or margarine, softened
¾ cup brown sugar
3 eggs
¾ cup honey
2 teaspoons grated lemon rind
½ cup strong coffee
2 cups white flour

1½ cups whole wheat flour
2 teaspoons baking powder
1 teaspoon baking soda
¼ teaspoon salt
1 teaspoon cinnamon
¾ teaspoon nutmeg
2 cups peeled, cored, and chopped apples
½ cup coarsely chopped walnuts

1. In a large bowl, cream the butter or margarine with the brown sugar. Beat in the eggs, then the honey, lemon rind, and coffee.
2. In another bowl, stir together the flours, baking powder, baking soda, salt, cinnamon, and nutmeg. Beat into the creamed mixture. Stir in the apples and walnuts.
3. Turn the batter into a greased and floured tube pan. Bake the cake in a 350° oven for 1 hour and 10 minutes, or until it tests done with a toothpick. Let cool on a rack.

YIELD: 16 servings

APPLE SOUR CREAM STREUSEL CAKE

Here's a most attractive tube cake that's filled with tender apple slices and cinnamony-sweet streusel. Rich sour cream makes for a fine-textured cake that's a perfect go-with for coffee.

Cake Batter:

¾ cup (1½ sticks) butter or margarine, softened
1 cup granulated sugar
3 eggs
1 cup sour cream
1 teaspoon vanilla

3 cups flour
¼ teaspoon salt
4 teaspoons baking powder
2 apples, peeled and sliced
2 tablespoons apple jelly

Streusel: (Mix all ingredients together until crumbly)

½ cup flour
¼ teaspoon baking powder
2 teaspoons cinnamon
¾ cup brown sugar

2 tablespoons butter or margarine, softened
¼ cup finely chopped walnuts

1. In a large bowl, cream the butter or margarine with the granulated sugar. Beat in the eggs, then the sour cream and vanilla.

2. In another bowl, stir together the flour, salt, and baking powder. Beat into the creamed mixture.
3. Turn half the batter into a greased and floured tube pan. Sprinkle with half the streusel mixture. Lay the apple slices on top and dot with the jelly. Cover with the remaining batter and sprinkle with the remaining streusel.
4. Bake the cake in a 350° oven for 1 hour, or until it tests done with a toothpick. Transfer to a rack to cool.

YIELD: 16 servings

FRESH APPLE SPICE CAKE

Fresh apples become chunky applesauce in this exceptionally moist and dark spice cake. The cake is deliciously hearty—just right for a fall dessert.

4 cups peeled, cored, and sliced apples
1 cup water
2½ cups plus 2 tablespoons sugar, divided usage
1 cup plus 6 tablespoons (2¾ sticks) butter or margarine, softened
4 eggs

3 cups white flour
2 cups whole wheat flour
2 teaspoons baking soda
2 teaspoons cinnamon
½ teaspoon nutmeg
½ teaspoon ground cloves
¼ teaspoon salt
1 cup raisins

1. Place apples, water, and 2 tablespoons sugar in a saucepan. Cook, covered, over medium heat until tender, about 5 to 10 minutes. Set aside.
2. In a large bowl, cream the butter with the remaining 2½ cups sugar. Beat in the eggs, then the apple mixture, including the liquid.

3. In another bowl, stir together the flours, baking soda, spices, and salt. Beat into the apple mixture just until thoroughly moistened. Stir in the raisins.
4. Turn the batter into a greased and floured tube pan. Bake the cake in a 325° oven for 1½ hours, or until it tests done with a toothpick. Let cool on a rack.

YIELD: 20 to 24 servings

Cakes
With Applesauce

Applesauce makes for a hearty, moist cake. As I stated in the introduction to this chapter, store-bought applesauce is more convenient for baking purposes, although the flavor is less full-bodied than if you make your own.

If you would like *to make your own applesauce*, either for cakes or for just plain good eating, here's what to do: Peel, core, and thickly slice enough apples to about halfway fill whatever saucepan you will be using to cook them. Add 1 to 2 inches of water to the pot. Simmer the apples, covered, until they are very tender. Puree the apples in a blender, food processor, or ricer. For chunkier applesauce, just mash them with a fork. The sauce may be left unsweetened, or add sugar or honey to taste. That's all there is to it.

APPLESAUCE LOAF

A classic applesauce cake that's moist, spicy, and chock-full of raisins and nuts.

½ cup (1 stick) butter or
   margarine, softened
½ cup granulated sugar
½ cup brown sugar
1 egg
1 cup homemade or store-
   bought applesauce,
   sweetened or unsweetened

1⅔ cups flour
¼ teaspoon salt
1 teaspoon baking soda
1 teaspoon cinnamon
½ teaspoon ground cloves
1 cup raisins
1 cup coarsely chopped
   walnuts

1. In a bowl, cream the butter or margarine with the sugars. Beat in the egg, then the applesauce.
2. In another bowl, stir together the flour, salt, baking soda, and spices. Beat into the applesauce mixture and then stir in the raisins and walnuts.
3. Turn the batter into a greased and floured 9" x 5" loaf pan. Bake the cake in a 350° oven for 40 minutes, or until it tests done with a toothpick. Transfer to a rack to cool.

YIELD: 8 to 10 slices

APPLESAUCE–CRANBERRY SAUCE CAKE

This delightfully fruity cake is quickly put together with two convenience foods—store-bought applesauce and cranberry sauce (although you can certainly use homemade if you prefer). Rolled oats and spices add to its wholesome good taste.

½ cup (1 stick) butter or margarine, softened
1 cup brown sugar
2 eggs
1 cup applesauce, sweetened or unsweetened
¾ cup whole-berry cranberry sauce

¾ cup whole wheat flour
¾ cup white flour
¾ teaspoon baking soda
¼ teaspoon salt
1 teaspoon cinnamon
½ teaspoon ground cloves
¼ teaspoon nutmeg
1 cup rolled oats

1. In a large bowl, cream the butter with the brown sugar. Beat in the eggs, then the applesauce and cranberry sauce.
2. In another bowl, stir together the flours, baking soda, salt, spices, and oats. Beat into the creamed mixture.

3. Turn the batter into a greased and floured 8" x 10" baking pan. Bake in a 350° oven for 45 minutes, or until the cake tests done with a toothpick. Let cool on a rack.
YIELD: 12 servings

APPLESAUCE RUM-RAISIN CAKE

Lots of raisins soaked in rum turn this into a deluxe version of a timeless favorite. Try to soak the raisins overnight—if you don't have the time, though, an hour or two will do.

½ cup golden raisins
½ cup dark raisins
⅓ cup dark rum
½ cup (1 stick) butter or margarine, softened
1 cup sugar
2 eggs
1½ cups homemade or store-bought applesauce, sweetened or unsweetened
1 cup white flour

1 cup whole wheat flour
1 tablespoon cornstarch
2 teaspoons baking soda
1 teaspoon cinnamon
½ teaspoon nutmeg
¼ teaspoon salt
1 tablespoon cocoa, sifted if lumpy
½ cup coarsely chopped walnuts

---

1. Place the raisins in a small bowl with the rum and let sit overnight, if possible.
2. In a large bowl, cream the butter or margarine with the sugar. Beat in the eggs, then the applesauce.
3. In another bowl, stir together the flours, cornstarch, baking soda, spices, salt, and cocoa. Beat into the creamed ingredients. Stir in the raisins, along with any rum that was not absorbed, and the walnuts.

4. Turn the batter into a greased and floured 9" x 13" baking pan. Bake the cake in a 375° oven for 25 minutes, or until it tests done with a toothpick. Let cool on a rack.
YIELD: 12 servings

APPLESAUCE OATMEAL CAKE

Here's a hearty cake that combines the moistness of applesauce with the wholesomeness and chewiness of oats. It's a marvelous gift cake and also a great bring-along for picnics.

¾ cup (1½ sticks) butter or margarine, softened
1½ cups sugar
4 eggs
1 cup plus 2 tablespoons homemade or store-bought applesauce, sweetened or unsweetened
¾ cup milk
1½ cups flour

1½ cups rolled oats
¼ teaspoon salt
1 tablespoon baking powder
1½ teaspoons cinnamon
¾ teaspoon nutmeg
¾ teaspoon ground cloves
1½ cups raisins
1½ cups coarsely chopped walnuts or pecans

1. In a large bowl, cream the butter or margarine with the sugar. Beat in the eggs, then the applesauce and milk.
2. In another bowl, stir together the flour, oats, salt, baking powder, and spices. Beat into the applesauce mixture. Stir in the raisins and nuts.
3. Turn the batter into a greased and floured tube pan. Bake the cake in a 350° oven for 65 minutes, or until it tests done with a toothpick. Let cool on a rack.
YIELD: 16 servings

APPLESAUCE RAISIN BRAN CAKE

This hearty, homey spice cake is quickly put together and makes a fine dessert, particularly during the winter months.

1¼ cups milk
1 cup whole bran cereal,
   such as All-Bran
2 eggs
1 cup sugar
¾ cup (1½ sticks) butter or
   margarine, melted
¾ cup homemade or store-
   bought applesauce,
   preferably unsweetened

1½ cups white flour
1 cup whole wheat flour
1 tablespoon baking powder
1 teaspoon baking soda
2 teaspoons cinnamon
1 teaspoon nutmeg
½ teaspoon salt
⅔ cup raisins

---

1. In a small bowl, soak the bran cereal in the milk for 5 minutes.
2. Meanwhile, beat the eggs slightly. Gradually beat in the sugar. When done, the mixture should be thick and pale. Beat in the melted butter or margarine. Then beat in the applesauce and bran, along with any milk that was not absorbed.
3. In another bowl, stir together the flours, baking powder, baking soda, cinnamon, nutmeg, and salt. Beat into the bran mixture and then stir in the raisins.
4. Turn the batter into a greased and floured tube pan. Bake the cake in a 325° oven for 1 hour and 20 minutes, or until it tests done with a toothpick. Transfer to a rack to cool.

YIELD: 16 servings

APPLESAUCE MOLASSES CAKE

Here's a hearty old-fashioned molasses cake with plenty of flavor from the fruity applesauce. It's a quick-to-make, quick-to-bake cake that can be eaten as soon as it comes from the oven. For an extra treat, top each serving with a spoonful of applesauce.

½ cup (1 stick) butter or
 margarine, softened
1 cup molasses
1 egg
1 cup homemade or store-
 bought applesauce,
 sweetened or unsweetened

2¼ cups flour
¼ teaspoon salt
1 teaspoon baking soda
1 teaspoon cinnamon
¾ cup raisins

1. In a bowl, cream the butter or margarine with the molasses. Beat in the egg, then the applesauce.
2. In another bowl, stir together the flour, salt, baking soda, and cinnamon. Beat into the applesauce mixture, then stir in the raisins.
3. Turn the batter into a greased and floured 8" x 8" baking pan. Bake the cake in a 350° oven for 40 minutes, or until it tests done with a toothpick. Let cool on a rack.

YIELD: 9 servings

PEANUT BUTTER APPLESAUCE CAKE

Apples and peanuts have always been a great combination for snacking. Here, applesauce and peanut butter pair up with equally felicitous results. This is one of those homey cakes that's perfect for any-time munching.

4 tablespoons (½ stick) butter or margarine, softened
½ cup peanut butter, preferably chunk style
1 cup sugar
1 egg
1 cup homemade or store-bought applesauce, sweetened or unsweetened

1¼ cups flour
1 teaspoon baking soda
¼ teaspoon salt
½ teaspoon cinnamon
¼ teaspoon nutmeg
¼ teaspoon ground cloves

1. In a bowl, cream the butter and peanut butter with the sugar. Beat in the egg, then the applesauce.
2. In another bowl, stir together the flour, baking soda, salt, and spices. Beat into the applesauce mixture.
3. Turn the batter into a greased and floured 8" x 8" baking pan. Bake in a 350° oven for 35 minutes, or until the cake tests done with a toothpick. Let cool on a rack.

YIELD: 9 servings

Cakes With Bananas

If you are planning to bake a banana cake, buy your fruit several days in advance so it will have plenty of time to ripen. Brown-flecked, quite soft bananas are sweetest in flavor and aroma and impart a delectable quality to baked goods. Of course, if you have overripe bananas already on hand, they need not go to waste when you remember how good the meltingly tender fruit will be when baked up into a cake.

BANANA CHOCOLATE CHIP CAKE

Chopped milk chocolate bars fleck this always-popular banana loaf.

½ cup (1 stick) butter or
   margarine, softened
¾ cup sugar
2 eggs
1 teaspoon vanilla
1 cup mashed ripe bananas

2 cups flour
¼ teaspoon salt
1 teaspoon baking soda
6 1-ounce milk chocolate
   bars, coarsely chopped

1. In a bowl, cream the butter or margarine with the sugar. Beat in the eggs, then the vanilla and mashed bananas.
2. In another bowl, stir together the flour, salt, and baking soda. Beat into the banana mixture and then stir in the chocolate.

3. Turn the batter into a greased and floured 9" x 5" loaf pan. Bake the cake in a 350° oven for 1 hour, or until it tests done with a toothpick. Transfer to a rack to cool.
YIELD: 8 to 10 slices

BANANA CRUMB CAKE

Soft, moist banana chunks flavor this economical cake that's simply wonderful served warm right from the oven. The cake is hearty, wholesome, and not too sweet—perfect for a weekend coffee cake breakfast. As with all banana cakes, the riper the bananas, the more flavorful the cake. However, because for this recipe the bananas are in chunks rather than mashed, if they are less ripe than ideal, the cake will still be fine.

Cake Batter:

6 tablespoons butter or margarine, softened
¾ cup granulated sugar
1 egg
grated rind from 1 lemon
1 teaspoon vanilla
1 cup milk

1 cup white flour
1 cup whole wheat flour
2 teaspoons baking powder
⅛ teaspoon salt
2 cups coarsely chopped bananas

Crumb Topping: (Mix together all ingredients until crumbly)

4 tablespoons butter or margarine, softened
⅓ cup flour
⅓ cup brown sugar

¾ teaspoon cinnamon
½ cup coarsely chopped pecans

1. In a large bowl, cream the butter or margarine with the granulated sugar. Beat in the egg, then the lemon rind, vanilla, and milk.

2. In another bowl, stir together the flours, baking powder, and salt. Beat into the creamed mixture and then stir in the bananas.
3. Spread the batter evenly in a greased and floured 8" x 10" baking pan. Sprinkle with the crumb topping.
4. Bake the cake in a 375° oven for about 45 minutes, or until it tests done with a toothpick. Let the pan cool on a rack.

YIELD: 12 servings

GINGERED BANANA CAKE

Crystallized ginger adds a pleasant contrast to the mellow banana flavor in this hearty, whole wheat ring cake. It's simple to whip up and makes a homey dessert on a winter night.

1 cup (2 sticks) butter or margarine, softened
1½ cups sugar
4 eggs
1¼ cups mashed ripe bananas
⅓ cup sour cream

1 teaspoon vanilla
1½ cups white flour
1 cup whole wheat flour
1 teaspoon baking powder
⅓ cup finely diced crystallized ginger

1. In a large bowl, cream the butter or margarine with the sugar. Beat in the eggs, then the bananas, sour cream, and vanilla.
2. In another bowl, stir together the flours and baking powder. Beat into the creamed mixture and then stir in the ginger.
3. Turn the batter into a greased and floured tube pan. Bake the cake in a 350° oven for about 1¼ hours, or until it tests done with a toothpick. Let cool on a rack.

YIELD: 16 servings

BANANA OATMEAL CRUMB CAKE

This is a luscious cake, full of rich banana flavor. The baked-on oatmeal crumb topping makes it especially inviting.

Cake Batter:

½ cup (1 stick) butter or margarine, softened
⅔ cup brown sugar
2 eggs
1 cup mashed ripe bananas

1 teaspoon vanilla
¾ cup flour
1⅓ cups rolled oats
¼ teaspoon salt
1 teaspoon baking soda

Topping: (Mix all ingredients together until crumbly)

¾ cup rolled oats
⅓ cup brown sugar
2 tablespoons melted butter or margarine

2 tablespoons finely chopped walnuts
½ teaspoon cinnamon

---

1. In a bowl, cream the butter or margarine with the brown sugar. Beat in the eggs, then the bananas and vanilla.
2. In another bowl, stir together the flour, oats, salt, and baking soda. Beat into the banana mixture.
3. Turn the batter into a greased and floured 8" x 8" baking pan. Sprinkle with the topping mixture. Bake the cake in a 350° oven for 40 to 45 minutes, or until it tests done with a toothpick. Transfer to a rack to cool.

YIELD: 9 servings

TROPICAL BANANA CAKE

Bananas and crushed pineapple flavor this fruity cake that tastes of the Caribbean. It's an easily prepared tube cake that's perfect for any special gathering.

1 cup (2 sticks) butter or
   margarine, softened
3 eggs
2 cups sugar
½ cup milk
1½ teaspoons vanilla
1 can (about 8 ounces)
   crushed pineapple,
   preferably juice-pack,
   undrained

3 cups flour
1 teaspoon baking soda
¼ teaspoon salt
1 teaspoon cinnamon
2 bananas, diced

1. In a large bowl, cream together the butter or margarine and the sugar. Beat in the eggs, then the milk, vanilla, and pineapple, along with the juice from the can.
2. In another bowl, stir together the flour, baking soda, salt, and cinnamon. Beat into the creamed mixture. Stir in the bananas.
3. Turn the batter into a greased and floured tube pan. Bake in a 350° oven for 1 hour and 10 minutes, or until the cake tests done with a toothpick. Let cool on a rack.

YIELD: 16 servings

Cakes With Berries

Blueberries in the summer and cranberries throughout the fall and winter make marvelous additions to cakes, with their brilliant colors and wonderfully fruity flavors.

Blueberries go right into a cake batter with nothing more required than a rinsing in water and a quick check for any stems or unripe or spoiled berries.

Cranberries, on the other hand, must be either chopped or cooked for the full, tart flavor to penetrate the cake batter (of course, again you'll want to check for any stems or bad berries). Most of the cranberry cakes in this section, as well as the cranberry breads and bars in other chapters of the book, call for fresh, chopped berries, a task that's far more easily done in the blender or food processor than by hand. Some recipes do, however, specify cranberry sauce. While canned sauce has the obvious advantage of every-ready convenience, homemade cranberry sauce is so quickly prepared, you may prefer to make it and reap the benefits of its delightfully tart flavor.

To make cranberry sauce, combine in a saucepan 1 pound (4 cups) cranberries, 1½ cups water, and 2 cups sugar. Cook, uncovered, over a fairly high heat until the cranberries pop, about 10 mintues. This recipe may be halved. Two cups of homemade sauce is equal to one 1-pound can of whole-berry cranberry sauce.

BLUEBERRY WHIPPED CREAM CAKE

Whipped cream makes this cake, flavored with dark, juicy blueberries and ground walnuts, exceptionally light, yet rich. Topped with a scoop of vanilla ice cream, the cake is a refreshing dessert on any hot summer's eve.

1 cup heavy or whipping
   cream
2 eggs
1 cup sugar
1½ teaspoons vanilla
1 cup flour

1½ teaspoons baking powder
¼ teaspoon salt
¾ cup finely ground
   walnuts
⅔ cup blueberries

---

1. In a bowl, beat the cream until is is stiffly whipped. Set aside.
2. In another bowl, beat the eggs (no need to wash the beaters). Gradually beat in the sugar. When done, the mixture should be thick and pale. Beat in the vanilla.
3. In another bowl, stir together the flour, baking powder, and salt. Stir these dry ingredients into the egg mixture. Fold in the whipped cream gently but thoroughly and then fold in the nuts.
4. Spread the batter evenly in an 8" x 10" baking pan. Sprinkle with the blueberries. Bake the cake in a 350° oven for 35 minutes, or until it tests done with a toothpick. Transfer to a rack to cool.

YIELD: 8 servings

BLUEBERRY CREAM CHEESE CAKE

This is my husband's favorite cake, and I make it for him each summer as soon as blueberries come into season. The cake itself tastes like a luscious, sweet, crumbly blueberry muffin, and is topped with a rich cream cheese filling that's covered with a delightful crumb mixture. As a coffee cake for breakfast or brunch, this one can't be beat. For dessert, try topping each square with a scoop of vanilla ice cream. When blueberries aren't available, finely diced, peeled, and cored apples may be substituted.

NOTE: Although there are three different mixtures to prepare for this cake, there's no need to wash the beaters between them. As another way of saving time, measure all the ingredients that go into all three mixtures into the different bowls at the same time (i.e., when you are adding sugar to the cake batter, add sugar to the bowl for the cream cheese filling and to the bowl for the crumb mixture, also).

Cake Batter:
⅓ cup (5⅓ tablespoons) butter
   or margarine, softened
⅓ cup sugar
2 eggs
¾ cup milk
¾ cup white flour
¾ cup whole wheat flour
1 tablespoon baking powder
¼ teaspoon salt
2 cups blueberries, divided
   usage

Cream Cheese Mixture: (Mix all ingredients together well)
1 3-ounce package cream
   cheese, softened
2 tablespoons sugar
1 tablespoon lemon juice

Crumb Topping: (Mix all ingredients together until crumbly)
½ cup white flour
½ cup whole wheat flour
¼ cup sugar
2 tablespoons butter or
   margarine, softened
¼ teaspoon cinnamon

1. In a bowl, cream the butter with the sugar. Beat in the eggs, then the milk.
2. In another bowl, stir together the flours, baking powder, and salt. Beat into the creamed mixture and then stir in 1 cup of the blueberries.
3. Turn the batter into a greased and floured 8" x 10" baking pan. Sprinkle with the remaining 1 cup blueberries. Drop tiny spoonfuls of the cream cheese mixture all over the top and sprinkle with the crumb mixture.
4. Bake the cake in a 375° oven for 30 minutes, or until it tests done with a toothpick. Transfer to a rack to cool. NOTE: Because this cake is so moist and fruity, it should be stored in the refrigerator.

YIELD: 12 servings

BLUEBERRY ALMOND LOAF

Here's a rich, dense blueberry loaf that's coated with plenty of crunchy almonds.

2 whole eggs
2 egg yolks
1 cup sugar
½ cup (1 stick) butter or margarine, melted
½ teaspoon vanilla
½ teaspoon grated lemon rind
1 cup plus 2 tablespoons flour

2 tablespoons cornstarch
⅛ teaspoon nutmeg
½ cup blueberries, tossed with 1½ tablespoons flour
¼ cup slivered blanched almonds

1. In a bowl, beat the whole eggs with the egg yolks. Gradually beat in the sugar until the mixture is thick and pale. Beat in the melted butter or margarine, vanilla, and lemon rind.
2. In another bowl, stir together the flour, cornstarch, and nutmeg. Beat into the egg mixture. Stir in the blueberries.

3. Grease and flour a 9" x 5" loaf pan and sprinkle the almonds evenly over the bottom. Turn the batter into the pan and bake the cake in a 350° oven for 45 minutes, or until it tests done with a toothpick. Let cool on a rack.

YIELD: 8 slices

CRANBERRY MOLASSES CAKE

Here's a moist, dark cranberry cake that makes a perfect fall family dessert. Leftovers are equally welcome as lunchbox treats.

1 cup cranberries
1 cup sugar, divided usage
½ cup (1 stick) butter or margarine, softened
¼ cup molasses
2 eggs
1 tablespoon vinegar plus enough milk to equal 1 cup liquid

1 tablespoon grated orange rind
1 cup whole wheat flour
1⅓ cups white flour
2 teaspoons baking powder
1 teaspoon baking soda
¼ teaspoon salt
½ cup coarsely chopped walnuts

1. Combine the cranberries and ¼ cup of the sugar in the blender or food processor and chop coarsely. (If you own neither of these appliances, simply chop the cranberries by hand and stir in the sugar.) Set aside.
2. In a large bowl, cream the butter or margarine with the remaining ¾ cup sugar. Beat in the molasses and eggs, then the vinegar-milk mixture and orange rind.
3. In another bowl, stir together the flours, baking powder, baking soda, and salt. Beat into the creamed mixture, then stir in the cranberries and walnuts.

4. Turn the batter into a greased and floured tube pan. Bake the cake in a 350° oven for 50 minutes, or until it tests done with a toothpick. Transfer to a rack to cool.

YIELD: 12 servings

UPSIDE-DOWN CRANBERRY GINGERBREAD

Festive enough for any Thanksgiving celebration, this moist cake has a fresh cranberry-orange topping over a dark gingerbread batter. Serve warm or chilled, plain or with whipped cream.

Topping:

2 cups cranberries
¾ cup sugar
1 whole seedless orange, cut into eighths

¼ cup raisins
4 tablespoons (½ stick) butter or margarine, melted

Cake Batter:

½ cup (1 stick) butter or margarine, softened
1 cup sugar
2 eggs
1 cup molasses
1 tablespoon lemon juice plus enough milk to equal 1 cup liquid
1 cup white flour

1 cup whole wheat flour
1 tablespoon cocoa, sifted if necessary
2 teaspoons baking soda
2 teaspoons cinnamon
1½ teaspoons ginger
¼ teaspoon nutmeg
¼ teaspoon salt

1. Place cranberries, sugar, and orange in a blender or food processor and process until finely chopped. Stir in the raisins. Spread the melted butter evenly in a 9" x 13" baking pan and top with the cranberry mixture.

2. In a bowl, cream the butter or margarine with the sugar. Beat in the eggs, then the molasses and lemon-milk mixture.
3. In another bowl, stir together the flours, cocoa, baking soda, spices, and salt. Beat into the creamed mixture.
4. Spread the batter over the cranberry mixture in the pre-pared pan. Bake the cake in a 350° oven for 45 minutes, or until it tests done with a toothpick. Invert the cake onto an ovenproof platter or baking sheet and bake 5 minutes longer. Transfer to a rack to cool. NOTE: If keeping the cake for longer than a day to two, store it in the refrigerator.

YIELD: 20 servings

CRANBERRY OATMEAL COBBLER-CAKE

A cross between a sweet, fruity cake and an old-fashioned cobbler, this dessert has a most pleasing homey quality. The oats lend a chewy texture that's delicious in both the crust and topping. This cake is delicious served warm or chilled, plain or with a scoop of ice cream or whipped cream.

3 cups cranberries
1 cup water
1¼ cups sugar, divided usage
¾ cups (1½ sticks) butter or margarine, softened
2 eggs

1 teaspoon vanilla
¾ cup white flour
½ cup whole wheat flour
1½ cups rolled oats
½ teaspoon baking powder
¼ teaspoon salt

1. Place cranberries and water in a saucepan. Cook until the cranberries pop. Drain and then stir in ¼ cup sugar.
2. In a bowl, cream the butter or margarine with the remaining 1 cup sugar. Beat in the eggs and vanilla.
3. In another bowl, stir together the flours, oats, baking powder, and salt. Beat into the creamed mixture.

4. Grease and flour an 8" x 10" baking pan. Reserving 1 cup of the batter, spread the rest evenly in the pan. Cover with the cranberries. Top with the reserved batter, in small spoonfuls. The cranberries will not be fully covered.
5. Bake the cake in a 350° oven for 45 minutes. Transfer to a rack to cool. NOTE: Store this cake in the refrigerator because it is so moist.

YIELD: 10 servings

CRANBERRY RUM-RAISIN BARS

These bars will serve you well during the holiday season, either for gift-giving or for your own enjoyment. The brown sugar lends a slight butterscotch flavor, which contrasts delightfully with the tart cranberries.

⅓ cup raisins
¼ cup dark rum
2 eggs
1½ cups brown sugar
½ cup (1 stick) butter or
   margarine, melted

1 teaspoon vanilla
1⅔ cups cranberries
⅓ cup walnuts
1½ cups flour
½ teaspoon baking powder
¼ teaspoon salt

1. In a small saucepan, simmer the raisins with the rum until the liquid has nearly evaporated.
2. In a blender or food processor, beat the eggs slightly. Add the brown sugar and process until the mixture is thick. Add the melted butter or margarine and process until incorporated. Add the cranberries and walnuts and process until coarsely chopped. If you own neither of these appliances, use an electric mixer and chop the cranberries by hand; you may purchase already-chopped walnuts.

3. In a bowl, stir together the flour, baking powder, and salt. Add the contents of the blender or food processor and stir well. Stir in the raisins.

4. Turn the batter into a greased and floured 9" x 13" baking pan. Bake the bars in a 350° oven for 50 minutes, or until they test done with a toothpick. Let cool on a rack and then cut into bars.

YIELD: 16

CRANBERRY–ORANGE CUPCAKES

These are a breeze to whip up with a blender or food processor but not so much fun with just a mixer, so if you lack these kitchen appliances you'd be best off skipping this recipe. These cupcakes are hearty, rich, and moist—perfect in the fall for brown-bag lunches. NOTE: Because cupcakes are so easily removed from tins, it's not necessary to flour the tins as long as you grease them thoroughly. Although paper cupcake liners make for easier clean-up, the deliciously crisp crust that normally forms on the sides and bottom of the cupcakes sticks to the liner, so we can't enjoy it.

½ cup (1 stick) butter or margarine, softened
⅔ cup sugar
1 whole orange
1 egg
⅓ cup orange juice

1 cup cranberries
1 cup whole wheat flour
½ cup white flour
1 teaspoon baking powder
½ teaspoon baking soda
¼ teaspoon salt

1. In the container of the blender or food processor, place the butter or margarine, cut into 4 pieces, the sugar, and the outer orange-colored rind of the orange (remove it with a vegetable peeler). Process until smooth.

2. Add the egg and blend in well. Discard the white membrane of the orange and add the segments to the blender or food processor, first removing any seeds. Process until smooth. Add the orange juice and cranberries and process until the cranberries are coarsely chopped.
3. In a bowl, stir together the flours, baking powder, baking soda, and salt. Add the contents of the blender or food processor and stir until the dry ingredients are moistened.
4. Spoon the batter into well-greased muffin tins, filling them nearly full. Bake the cupcakes in a 400° oven for about 20 minutes, or until they test done with a toothpick. Remove cupcakes from the tins and let cool on a rack.

YIELD: About 1 dozen cupcakes

Cakes
With Citrus

These can be among the most economical of cakes. While lemon or orange juice may be added to the batter for extra flavor, most of these cakes rely on the rind to impart a lively taste. This being one part of the fruit we'd normally discard, adding it to cakes makes good sense.

NOTE: Except in instances when the entire peel is specified, as in the candied orange peel recipe below, only the thin outer skin (the part that contains the color) of oranges and lemons should be used in recipes. This part contains the most flavor and is therefore appropriately termed "the zest."

If you have a blender or food processor, the lemon or orange rind can be most easily grated by simply removing it with a vegetable peeler and adding it to the machine along with the butter and sugar. Otherwise, a sturdy hand grater will serve you well. It is possible to purchase bottled lemon and orange rind in the spice section of the supermarket. However, I have found that in the drying process, the oils in these rinds are lost, along with much of their special flavor and zestiness.

Some recipes in this chapter and others throughout the book call for candied orange peel. This ingredient can be purchased in specialty or gourmet food stores. But it's easy to make your own; and, stored in the refrigerator, candied orange peel keeps for months.

ORANGE PECAN CAKE

Sour cream and pecans make this luscious orange cake one of the richest you'll ever encounter. It's also especially moist, since an orange liqueur mixture is poured over it after baking.

½ cup (1 stick) butter or margarine, softened
1 cup granulated sugar, divided usage
¾ cup brown sugar
2 eggs
1 teaspoon vanilla
1 cup sour cream
2 tablespoons grated orange rind

2 cups minus 2 tablespoons flour
¾ teaspoon baking powder
½ teaspoon baking soda
¼ teaspoon salt
¾ cup coarsely chopped pecans
¼ cup orange juice
2 tablespoons orange liqueur, such as Grand Marnier

1. In a large bowl, cream the butter or margarine with ¾ cup granulated sugar and the brown sugar. Beat in the eggs, then the vanilla, sour cream, and orange rind.
2. In another bowl, stir together the flour, baking powder, baking soda, and salt. Beat into the creamed mixture. Stir in the pecans.
3. Turn the batter into a greased and floured tube pan. Bake the cake in a 350° oven for 1 hour, or until it tests done with a toothpick. Just before it comes out of the oven, mix together the remaining ¼ cup sugar, the orange juice, and the liqueur. Pour over the baked cake. Transfer to a rack to cool.

YIELD: 14 to 16 servings

ORANGE JUICE CAKE

A cake flavored with orange juice concentrate—nothing could be faster or simpler. The juice drizzled over the cake after baking makes this low, oblong cake especially moist. Try it warm from the oven for a wonderful, quickly-prepared treat.

½ cup (1 stick) butter or
   margarine, softened
1 cup sugar
2 eggs
1 6-ounce can frozen orange
   juice concentrate, thawed,
   divided usage
½ cup milk
grated rind of 1 orange

2 cups flour
1 teaspoon baking soda
¼ teaspoon salt
1 cup currants (or substitute
   raisins, if preferred)
¼ cup finely chopped
   walnuts
⅓ cup sugar, mixed with 1
   teaspoon cinnamon

---

1. In a bowl, cream the butter or margarine with the sugar. Beat in the eggs, then ½ cup of the orange juice concentrate, and the milk and orange rind.
2. In another bowl, stir together the flour, baking soda, and salt. Beat into the orange mixture. Stir in the currants and walnuts.
3. Turn the batter into a greased and floured 9" x 13" baking pan. Bake the cake in a 350° oven for 30 minutes, or until it tests done with a toothpick. As soon as it comes from the oven, drizzle the remaining orange juice concentrate over the cake and sprinkle with the cinnamon-sugar mixture. Transfer to a rack to cool.

YIELD: 20 servings

ORANGE OATMEAL CAKE

Here's cake with the fresh piquancy of orange juice and the hearty chewiness of oats. Warm from the oven or cool, it makes a great any-time snack.

1 cup (2 sticks) butter or
　margarine, softened
½ cup brown sugar
½ cup granulated sugar
1 egg
½ cup orange juice
2 teaspoons vanilla
1 tablespoon grated orange
　rind

1½ cups flour
¾ cup rolled oats
¼ teaspoon salt
1 teaspoon ginger
1 teaspoon baking powder
½ cup coarsely chopped
　nuts

------

1. In a large bowl, cream the butter or margarine with the sugars. Beat in the egg, then the orange juice, vanilla, and orange rind.
2. In another bowl, stir together the flour, oats, salt, ginger, and baking powder. Beat into the orange mixture and then stir in the nuts.
3. Turn the batter into a greased and floured 9" x 13" baking pan. Bake the cake in a 350° oven for 40 minutes, or until it tests done with a toothpick. Transfer to a rack to cool.

YIELD: 16 to 20 servings

ORANGE ALMOND TEA LOAF

A not-too-sweet loaf, a perfect offering for tea or brunch. Orange juice and rind, along with crunchy almonds and dark rum, flavor this rich, dense cake.

⅝ cup (1¼ sticks) butter or margarine, softened
¾ cup sugar
3 eggs
2 tablespoons orange juice
2 tablespoons dark rum
1 tablespoon grated orange rind
1 cup plus 2 tablespoons flour

½ teaspoon baking powder
⅛ teaspoon salt
1 teaspoon ground coriander (or substitute cinnamon, if you prefer)
½ cup slivered, blanched almonds

---

1. In a bowl, cream the butter or margarine with the sugar. Beat in the eggs, then the orange juice, rum and orange rind.
2. In another bowl, stir together the flour, baking powder, salt, and coriander. Beat into the creamed mixture. Stir in the almonds.
3. Turn the batter into a greased and floured 9" x 5" loaf pan. Bake in a 350° oven for 45 minutes, or until the cake tests done with a toothpick. Let cool on a rack.

YIELD: 8 to 10 slices

CANDIED ORANGE PEEL

entire peel from 6 oranges,   1 cup sugar
  cut into ¼-inch strips

1. Place the peel in a saucepan. Cover with cold water, bring to a boil, and drain. Repeat two more times. Cover with cold water, bring to a boil, boil 1 minute, and drain.
2. Add the sugar and 2 tablespoons water to the saucepan with the peels. Simmer, stirring occasionally, about 20 minutes, or until the peel is almost dry.
3. Spread the peel on a baking sheet and place in a 200° oven until it is dry. Let cool and then store in the refrigerator in a glass jar.

YIELD: About 2½ cups candied orange peel

CANDIED ORANGE LOAF

This is a simple, economical cake that's perfect when you're in the mood for something that's not too sweet.

¼ cup (½ stick) butter or
  margarine, softened
½ cup sugar
3 eggs
1 tablespoon vinegar plus
  enough milk to equal 1
  cup liquid altogether

3 cups flour
1 tablespoon baking powder
½ teaspoon baking soda
¼ teaspoon salt
1½ cups diced candied
  orange peel

1. In a bowl, cream the butter or margarine with the sugar. Beat in the eggs, then the vinegar-milk mixture.
2. In another bowl, stir together the flour, baking powder, baking soda, and salt. Beat into the creamed mixture and then stir in the orange peel.

3. Turn the batter into a greased and floured 9" x 5" loaf pan. Bake the cake in a 325° oven for 1 hour, or until it tests done with a toothpick. Transfer to a rack to cool.

YIELD: 8 servings

LEMON LOAF

This is a simple, fresh-tasting loaf that, with its zesty lemon flavor, is perfect with afternoon tea. Sour cream gives it a light, yet rich texture.

5 tablespoons butter or
   margarine, softened
1½ cups sugar, divided usage
2 eggs
1 teaspoon vanilla
⅓ cup sour cream
2½ tablespoons milk
1½ cups flour

¼ teaspoon salt
1 teaspoon baking powder
⅓ cup finely chopped
   walnuts
unstrained juice of 1 lemon
(remove the seeds but keep the
flecks of lemon pulp)

1. In a bowl, cream the butter or margarine with 1 cup sugar. Beat in the eggs, then the vanilla, sour cream, and milk.
2. In another bowl, stir together the flour, salt, and baking powder. Beat into the creamed mixture and then stir in the walnuts.
3. Turn the batter into a greased and floured 9" x 5" loaf pan. Bake the cake in a 350° oven for 50 minutes, or until it tests done with a toothpick.
4. Meanwhile, mix together the remaining ½ cup sugar with the lemon juice. As soon as the cake comes from the oven, spoon this mixture evenly over the surface and let it sink in. Let the cake cool on a rack.

YIELD: 8 to 10 slices

SOUFFLÉED LEMON CAKE

This cake, calling for very little flour and a half-dozen eggs, is very rich and moist, almost custardlike in texture. It rises majestically during baking and then sinks as it cools, so don't be surprised at its 3-inch final height.

NOTE: It is essential that you use freshly squeezed lemon juice in the cake. The juice is reduced to give an intense lemon flavor that creates an almost bittersweet effect.

⅔ cup freshly squeezed
    lemon juice
6 eggs, separated
⅛ teaspoon cream of tartar
pinch salt
1 cup sugar

9 tablespoons (1 stick plus 1
    tablespoon) butter, melted
    (use real butter, if possible)
grated rind of 1 orange
¾ cup milk
⅔ cup flour

---

1. Place the lemon juice in a saucepan and boil until it is reduced to ¼ cup. Let cool.
2. In a bowl, beat the egg whites until stiff with the cream of tartar and salt, and set aside.
3. In another bowl, beat the egg yolks. Gradually beat in the sugar. When done, the mixture should be thick and pale. Beat in the melted butter, then the orange rind, lemon juice, and milk. Stir in the flour.
4. Stir about one-third of the egg whites into the batter and then fold in the rest gently but thoroughly.
5. Turn the batter into a greased and floured tube pan. Bake the cake in a 325° oven for 1¼ hours (when tested with a toothpick, it will test slightly underdone). Place on a rack and run a knife around the edges so that it can sink without tearing.

YIELD: **10 servings**

ALMOND LEMON CAKE

*This lemon cake has a delicate pale color because it con-
tains no egg yolks—only the whites. Yet because of the butter and sour cream, it's far richer than an angel food cake.
Altogether, the cake is delightful, with a lovely springlike feel-
ing to it.*

8 egg whites
pinch cream of tartar
1 cup sugar, divided usage
1 cup (2 sticks) butter,
  softened (use real butter, if
  possible)
grated rind of 1½ lemons
1 tablespoon lemon juice

1 cup sour cream
2 teaspoons vanilla
2 cups flour
1 teaspoon baking powder
⅛ teaspoon salt
1 cup finely chopped
  blanched almonds

1. In a bowl, beat the egg whites with the cream of tartar until
   stiff. Gradually beat in ½ cup of the sugar.
2. In a large bowl, cream the butter with the remaining sugar.
   Beat in the lemon rind, lemon juice, sour cream, and vanilla.
3. In another bowl, stir together the flour, baking powder, and
   salt. Stir the dry ingredients into the butter mixture, along
   with about one-third of the beaten egg whites. Fold in the
   rest of the egg whites gently but thoroughly. Stir in the
   almonds.
4. Turn the batter into a greased and floured tube pan. Bake
   the cake in a 350° oven for abour 1 hour and 10 minutes,
   or until it tests done with a toothpick. Let cool on a rack.

YIELD: 12 to 14 servings

LEMON CAKE

A lively fresh lemon syrup penetrates this lemon-and-brown-sugar-flavored cake. It's appealingly moist and not too sweet.

4 tablespoons butter or
  margarine, softened
1¼ cups brown sugar,
  divided usage
1 egg
2 teaspoons lemon juice
  plus enough milk to equal
  ¾ cup liquid

2 teaspoons grated lemon
  rind
1⅓ cups flour
⅛ teaspoon salt
1 teaspoon baking soda
1 tablespoon dark rum
3 tablespoons fresh lemon
  juice

1. In a bowl, cream the butter or margarine with 1 cup brown sugar. Beat in the egg, then the lemon-milk mixture and lemon rind.
2. In another bowl, stir together the flour, salt, and baking soda. Beat into the lemon mixture.
3. Turn the batter into a greased and floured 8" x 8" baking pan. Bake the cake in a 350° oven for 30 minutes, or until it tests done with a toothpick.
4. Meanwhile, combine the remaining ¼ cup brown sugar, and the rum and lemon juice in a small saucepan. Heat to boiling, stirring to dissolve the sugar. Pour the syrup evenly over the cake as soon as it comes from the oven. Let cool on a rack. This cake is even better on the second day, when the syrup has had time to penetrate fully into it.

YIELD: 9 servings

Cakes
With Other Fruits

Cake recipes calling for peaches, plums, pears, cherries, and the other fruits you'll find on the next several pages are less numerous, so I've grouped them all into a single section of this chapter. But when you bite into a piece of Upside-Down Peach Gingerbread, for example, you'll wonder at the scarcity of recipes using these fruits.

Part of the reason is probably that most of these fruits are seasonal and somewhat expensive. When cherries are available only two months a year and cost nearly a dollar a pound, it's hard to do anything with them but greedily pop them into your mouth.

Let me assure you, though, that any fruits you part with for cake baking will only increase in their pleasure-giving. For when you surround a morsel of fruit with a delectable cake batter, you'll enhance its character rather than appreciably change its flavor. Thus, the Santa Rosa Plum Cake tastes of juicy plums, the Cherry Almond Cake of red ripe cherries, and the Peach-Filled Cake of tender peaches. All that's added is some great-tasting cake.

UPSIDE-DOWN PEACH GINGERBREAD

As you may see from the number of upside-down cake recipes in this book, they are one of my favorite types of cake. They are always most attractive and so are perfect for party fare, while also providing plenty of family enjoyment. This version perches delectable fresh peaches on a spicy gingerbread cake. The golden fruit makes a pleasing contrast to the dark brown batter.

1 cup (2 sticks) butter or margarine, divided usage	½ cup molasses
1 cup brown sugar	grated rind from ½ lemon
2 tablespoons honey	1 cup white flour
2½ cups peeled peach slices	1 cup whole wheat flour
½ cup coarsely chopped pecans	1½ teaspoons ginger
1 cup granulated sugar	1 teaspoon nutmeg
2 eggs	1 teaspoon baking soda
	¼ teaspoon salt
	½ cup boiling water

1. Melt ½ cup (1 stick) of the butter or margarine in a heavy 10-inch skillet with an ovenproof handle. Tilt to grease the sides of the skillet. Stir in the brown sugar and honey until dissolved and spread to coat the bottom of the skillet evenly. Arrange the peach slices in the skillet in an attractive pattern and sprinkle with the pecans. Set aside.
2. In a bowl, cream the remaining ½ cup butter or margarine with the granulated sugar. Beat in the eggs, then the molasses and lemon rind.
3. In another bowl, stir together the flours, ginger, nutmeg, baking soda, and salt. Beat into the creamed mixture, along with the boiling water.
4. Turn the batter carefully into the prepared skillet. Bake the cake in a 350° oven for 45 minutes, or until it tests done with a toothpick. Run a knife around the edge and tip the cake upside down onto an ovenproof platter. Bake the cake 5 to 10 minutes longer, or until the topping is set. Transfer to a rack to cool. NOTE: Because this cake is so moist, it should be stored in the refrigerator.

YIELD: 12 servings

PEACH GRAHAM UPSIDE-DOWN TORTE

Graham cracker crumbs replace the customary flour in this summery light torte. Fresh peaches look ever-so-appealing when the finished cake is turned upside down out of the baking pan. Serve this cake warm or cold, for breakfast or brunch or topped with a scoop of peach or vanilla ice cream for dessert.

9 tablespoons (1 stick plus 1 tablespoon) butter or margarine, softened, divided usage
1 tablespoon brown sugar
4 peaches, peeled and sliced
3 eggs, separated
¾ cup granulated sugar
¾ cup milk

1 teaspoon vanilla
2 cups finely crushed graham cracker crumbs (use either packaged crumbs or a rolling pin, blender, or food processor to make your own)
1 teaspoon baking powder
⅛ teaspoon salt

1. Place 1 tablespoon butter or margarine in an 8" to 10" baking pan. Place the pan in the oven as you preheat it to 375°. When the butter has melted, remove the pan from the oven and stir the brown sugar into the butter. Spread to coat the bottom evenly. Arrange the peaches in the pan, and set aside.
2. In a small bowl, beat the egg whites until stiff, and set aside.
3. In a bowl, cream the remaining 8 tablespoons butter or margarine with the granulated sugar. Beat in the egg yolks, then the milk and vanilla.
4. In another bowl, stir together the graham cracker crumbs, baking powder, and salt. Beat into the creamed mixture. Fold in the egg whites gently but thoroughly.
5. Turn the batter into the prepared pan. Bake in a 375° oven for 40 minutes, or until the cake tests done with a toothpick. Immediately invert the cake upside down onto a large plate. NOTE: Because this cake is so moist, it should be stored in the refrigerator.

YIELD: 8 servings

PEACH-FILLED CAKE

Here's a wonderful cake to enjoy in the middle of the summer, when the peach harvest is at its peak. A lovely, light lemon cake is filled with fresh peach slices, sweetened with brown sugar, and spiced with cinnamon. Plain or topped with ice cream, this is a lovely dessert for family and friends.

¾ cup (1½ sticks) butter or margarine, softened
1 cup granulated sugar
3 eggs
1 teaspoon grated lemon rind
⅔ cup milk
1 cup white flour
1 cup minus 2 tablespoons whole wheat flour
2 teaspoons baking powder
¼ teaspoon salt
4 medium-sized peaches, peeled and sliced (about 1½ cups slices)
⅓ cup brown sugar, mixed with ½ teaspoon cinnamon

---

1. In a bowl, cream the butter or margarine with the granulated sugar. Beat in the eggs, then the lemon rind and milk.
2. In another bowl, stir together the flours, baking powder, and salt. Beat into the creamed mixture.
3. Spread half the batter evenly in a greased and floured 8" x 10" baking pan. Arrange the peach slices on top and sprinkle with the brown sugar-cinnamon mixture. Spread the remaining batter on top.
4. Bake the cake in a 350° oven for 50 minutes, or until it tests done with a toothpick. Let cool on a rack. Because this cake is so moist, it is easiest to serve it directly from the baking pan. NOTE: It should be stored in the refrigerator.

YIELD: 16 servings

FRESH FRUIT FRUITCAKE

Fresh oranges (including the rind), bananas, and apples all go into this incredibly moist, fruity cake. NOTE: You need a food processor, blender, or manual grinder to chop the fruit finely enough.

2 oranges with rind on, cut into eighths and seeded
2 ripe bananas, peeled and cut into 2" lengths
2 apples, peeled, cored, and cut into eighths
2 eggs
1½ cups sugar

½ cup (1 stick) butter or margarine, melted
3 cups flour
1 tablespoon baking powder
2 teaspoons baking soda
½ cup raisins
½ cup coarsely chopped walnuts

---

1. Puree the oranges in a food processor, blender, or grinder until the rind is very finely chopped. Transfer to a bowl. Process the bananas until mashed. Remove to bowl with oranges. Then process the apples until very finely chopped. Add to bowl with other fruit.
2. In a large bowl, beat the eggs. Gradually beat in the sugar until the mixture is thick and pale. Beat in the melted butter or margarine and then the fruits.
3. In another bowl, stir together the flour, baking powder, and baking soda. Beat into the fruit mixture and then stir in the raisins and walnuts.
4. Turn the batter into a greased and floured 9" x 13" baking pan. Bake the cake in a 350° oven for 50 to 60 minutes, or until it tests done with a toothpick. Transfer to a rack to cool.

YIELD: 20 servings

CLASSIC PINEAPPLE UPSIDE-DOWN CAKE

This is the luscious pineapple upside-down cake we all remember from our childhoods (if we were so lucky). A rich, sweet, and deliciously sticky pineapple mixture forms the topping for a simple, light butter cake. To make this cake properly, you'll need a very heavy, deep 10" skillet, preferably cast iron, with an ovenproof handle.

1 20-ounce can sliced pineapple, preferably juice-packed (drain and reserve ¼ cup juice)
¾ cup (1½ sticks) butter or margarine, softened, divided usage
⅔ cup brown sugar
⅓ cup pecan halves
¾ cup granulated sugar
2 eggs
1 teaspoon vanilla
1 cup milk
2 cups flour
1 tablespoon baking powder
¼ teaspoon salt

1. In a heavy, deep 10-inch skillet, melt ¼ cup (½ stick) butter or margarine. Tilt the skillet to grease the sides of the pan. Add the brown sugar and stir until it is melted. Spread this mixture evenly along the bottom of the pan. Arrange the pineapple rings decoratively on the bottom and up the sides of the skillet (you may wish to cut some of the rings in half). Sprinkle with the pecans. Set aside.
2. In a bowl, cream the remaining ½ cup (1 stick) butter or margarine with the granulated sugar. Beat in the eggs, then the vanilla, milk, and reserved ¼ cup pineapple juice.
3. In another bowl, stir together the flour, baking powder, and salt. Beat into the creamed mixture.
4. Turn the batter carefully into the prepared skillet. Bake the cake in a 350° oven for 50 minutes, or until it tests done with a toothpick. Run a knife around the sides of the skillet. Turn out onto an ovenproof platter and bake the cake upside down for 5 minutes longer, or until the topping is set. Transfer to a rack to cool.

YIELD: 12 servings

PEAR CAKE

This is a lovely cake during the fall and winter months, when few fruits are available in the market. The pears add a very delicate flavor to this hearty oatmeal cake. NOTE: Use ripe but still fairly firm pears. Any variety will do fine— Bosc, Bartlett, Anjou, etc. Use the coarse edge of a hand grater to grate them.

4 eggs
1½ cups brown sugar
¾ cup (1½ stick) butter or
  margarine, melted
2 teaspoons vanilla
1½ cups white flour
1½ cups whole wheat flour

1 cup rolled oats
1 tablespoon baking powder
½ teaspoon baking soda
1½ teaspoons cinnamon
¼ teaspoon salt
1½ cups coarsely grated
  unpeeled pears

1. In a large bowl, beat the eggs. Gradually beat in the brown sugar until the mixture is thick. Beat in the melted butter or margarine and the vanilla.
2. In another bowl, stir together the flours, oats, baking powder, baking soda, cinnamon and salt. Beat into the liquid mixture and then stir in the pears.
3. Turn the batter into a greased and floured tube pan. Bake the cake in a 325° oven for 1 hour and 10 minutes, or until it tests done with a toothpick. Transfer to a rack to cool.

YIELD: 16 servings

GRAPE CUPCAKES

Fresh green seedless grapes, folded into a light cupcake, make for a lovely summer dessert, especially when accompanied by a dish of ice cream.

½ cup (1 stick) butter or
  margarine, softened
⅔ cup sugar
2 eggs
1 teaspoon vanilla
¾ cup white flour
¾ cup whole wheat flour

¼ teaspoon salt
1½ teaspoons baking
  powder
½ cup golden raisins
1 cup seedless green
  grapes, halved

1. In a bowl, cream the butter or margarine with the sugar. Beat in the eggs and vanilla.
2. In another bowl, stir together the flours, salt, and baking powder. Beat into the creamed mixture and then stir in the raisins and grapes.
3. Divide the batter among 10 greased and floured or paper-lined muffin tins. Bake the cupcakes in a 350° oven for 25 minutes, or until they test done with a toothpick. Immediately remove the cupcakes from the tins and let cool on a rack.

YIELD: 10 cupcakes

SPRINGTIME RHUBARB CAKE

There's almost more fruit than cake in this delightful spring-time dessert or brunch treat. Sour cream and brown sugar make for a delicious batter that holds tart and tangy rhubarb pieces.

4 tablespoons (½ stick)
  butter or margarine,
  softened
1¼ cups brown sugar
1 egg
1 8-ounce container sour
  cream

1 teaspoon vanilla
1 cup whole wheat flour
1⅓ cups white flour
1 teaspoon baking soda
¼ teaspoon nutmeg
⅛ teaspoon salt
4 cups rhubarb, in ½" dice

1. In a bowl, cream the butter or margarine with the brown sugar. Beat in the egg, then the sour cream and vanilla.
2. In another bowl, stir together the flours, baking soda, nutmeg, and salt. Beat into the creamed mixture and then stir in the rhubarb. (The batter will be quite stiff, but this is necessary since the rhubarb gives off some liquid while baking.)
3. Turn the batter into a greased and floured 9" x 13" baking pan. Bake the cake in a 350° oven for 45 to 50 minutes, or until it tests done with a toothpick. Let cool on a rack. NOTE: This cake should be stored in the refrigerator.

YIELD: 18 to 20 servings

SANTA ROSA PLUM CAKE

Here's a cake for those who complain that they can never finish a whole cake. Yielding just six servings, this plummy dessert is perfect for a small family or an intimate dinner party. Incidentally, Santa Rosa plums are red on the outside, yellow in the center, and very round and juicy. If they're unavailable, try substituting another variety.

3 eggs, separated
½ cup (1 stick) butter or
   margarine, softened
½ cup sugar
1 teaspoon grated lemon
   rind

1 cup flour
½ teaspoon baking powder
1¼ cups pitted and quartered
   Santa Rosa plums (about
   8 plums)

---

1. In a small bowl, beat the egg whites until stiff, and set aside.
2. In a large bowl, cream the butter or margarine with the sugar. Beat in the egg yolks and lemon rind.
3. Stir together the flour and baking powder and then beat

into the creamed mixture. Fold in the egg whites gently but thoroughly.
4. Spread the batter evenly in a greased and floured tube pan (there will be only a little over an inch of batter). Arrange the plums, skin side down, attractively over the batter.
5. Bake the cake in a 375° oven for 40 minutes, or until it tests done with a toothpick. Transfer to a rack to cool. NOTE: If you keep this cake for more than 24 hours, it should be refrigerated.

YIELD: 6 servings

CHERRY ALMOND CAKE

Here's a lovely, dense-textured cake with a strong almond flavor. Cherries dot the cake throughout, contributing an attractive color contrast.

1 1-pound can sweet, dark, pitted cherries, drained and soaked for 1 hour in ⅓ cup orange liqueur
1 cup (2 sticks) butter, softened (use real butter, if possible)
1 cup sugar

4 whole eggs plus 1 egg yolk
1 cup finely ground almonds
1 teaspoon vanilla
2 cups plus 2 tablespoons flour
4 teaspoons baking powder
⅛ teaspoon salt

1. In a large bowl, cream the butter with the sugar. Beat in the eggs and egg yolk, then the almonds and vanilla. Drain the cherries reserving the orange liqueur and beat it into the egg mixture.
2. In another bowl, stir together the flour, baking powder, and salt. Beat into the creamed mixture just until incorporated. Stir in the cherries, being careful not to crush them.

3. Turn the batter into a greased and floured 9" x 13" baking pan, making certain to distribute the cherries evenly. Bake the cake in a 350° oven for 45 minutes, or until it tests done with a toothpick. Let cool on a rack.
YIELD: 20 servings

PERSIMMON CAKE

This native American fruit remains exotic (and is rather expensive unless you grow your own). But if you have some gloriously orange persimmons on hand, they do bake up into an exceptionally dense and fine-flavored cake.

NOTE: Persimmons must be very ripe to be enjoyed. The texture will be much softer than that of a ripe peach; it will be almost meltingly soft when ready to eat or be used for baking. To make persimmon pulp, just cut the ripe fruit in half, remove any seeds, and scrape the fruit from the skin with a spoon. Mash with a fork.

2 eggs
1 cup sugar
5⅓ tablespoons butter or margarine, melted
1 cup ripe persimmon pulp (2 to 3 persimmons)

⅔ cup white flour
⅔ cup whole wheat flour
1½ teaspoons baking powder
1½ teaspoons cinnamon
⅛ teaspoon salt

1. Beat the eggs with the sugar until thick and pale-lemon-colored. Beat in the melted butter or margarine and then the persimmon pulp.
2. In another bowl, stir together the flours, baking powder, cinnamon, and salt. Beat into the persimmon mixture just until incorporated.
3. Turn the batter into a greased and floured 8" x 8" square pan. Bake in a 350° oven for 50 minutes, or until the cake tests done with a toothpick. Transfer to a rack to cool.
YIELD: 10 servings

Cakes With Vegetables

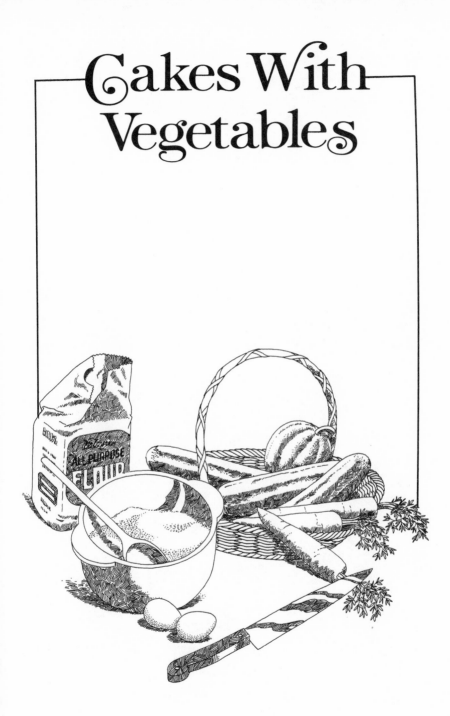

A decade or two ago, most people seeing this title would immediately turn up their noses in disdain. But suddenly, carrot cakes were "in." And after that, a variety of vegetable combinations—some delicious, others quite the opposite—started turning up in cakes everywhere. In this section you'll find a selection of the best of these vegetable cakes . . . featuring yams, white potatoes, zucchini, beets, pumpkin, and even sauerkraut.

The taste contributed to cakes by vegetables in usually quite negligible, so these batters are well-flavored with spices, orange rind, or cocoa. What the vegetables do add to cakes, though, is a most special texture. Cooked vegetables like pumpkin puree lend an exceptional moist quality, while grated raw vegetables like carrots add a hearty crunch.

Vegetables also lend a definite flair and vitality to any cake. Who, for example, could fail to be intrigued when you say, "Oh, you must sample my chocolate sauerkraut cake," or when you offhandedly remark, "By the way, the little green flecks aren't bits of mold; they're grated zucchini." These cakes not only taste great, but they will absolutely guarantee your reputation as a "with-it," innovative cook.

Cakes
With Carrots

Carrot cakes nearly always call for grated raw carrots. Of course, you may grate them by hand with a hand grater. But if you own a food processor, your work will be easier and speedier. I have found that the special grating blade makes carrot pieces that are too coarse and long. Also, it's bothersome to add the carrots through the feed tube. Try cutting the carrots into 1-inch lengths and using the steel blade instead; it will quickly mince the carrots as finely as if they had been grated by hand. Another option is to use a blender. Cut the peeled carrots into 1-inch lengths and add water to cover. Blend at high speed for a few seconds, until the carrots are finely minced. Pour into a colander immediately and let drain thoroughly.

NEW ENGLAND CARROT CAKE

Maple syrup from Vermont adds a unique flavor to this golden-orange carrot spice cake. With pecans and orange juice in the batter, it is a most special version of one of the most popular of all vegetable cakes.

½ cup (1 stick) butter or
  margarine, softened
¾ cup brown sugar
4 eggs
¾ cup real maple syrup
¾ cup orange juice
2 cups whole wheat flour
1¾ cups white flour
1 tablespoon baking powder

1 teaspoon baking soda
1 teaspoon cinnamon
½ teaspoon nutmeg
¼ teaspoon ginger
¼ teaspoon salt
½ cup coarsely chopped
  pecans
3 cups grated carrots

1. In a large bowl, cream the butter or margarine with the brown sugar. Beat in the eggs, then the maple syrup and orange juice.
2. In another bowl, stir together the flours, baking powder, baking soda, spices, and salt. Beat into the creamed mixture and then stir in the pecans and carrots.
3. Turn the batter into a greased and floured tube pan. Bake the cake in a 350° oven for 1 hour and 20 to 30 minutes, or until a toothpick inserted in the center comes out clean. Transfer to a rack to cool.

YIELD: 20 servings

SIMPLE CARROT LOAF

Here's a wholesome loaf that keeps well and is great for snacking any time of the day. The slight cooking of the carrots tends to enhance their flavor. This recipe is especially quick to fix because the butter is melted right into the grated carrots.

2 cups grated peeled carrots
½ cup (1 stick) butter or
  margarine, melted
¼ cup water
2 eggs
1 cup sugar
¾ cup white flour

½ cup whole wheat flour
1½ teaspoons cinnamon
1 teaspoon baking soda
1 teaspoon cloves
¾ teaspoon nutmeg
¼ teaspoon baking powder
¼ teaspoon salt

---

1. Place the carrots, butter or margarine, and water in a saucepan and bring to a boil. Simmer 5 minutes. Let cool while preparing the rest of the batter.
2. Beat the eggs in a large bowl. Gradually beat in the sugar until the mixture is thick and pale.
3. Stir together the remaining ingredients in another bowl. Beat the carrot mixture into the egg mixture and then beat in the dry ingredients.
4. Turn the batter into a greased and floured 9" x 5" loaf pan. Bake the cake in a 350° oven for about 50 minutes, or until it tests done with a toothpick. Transfer to a rack to cool.

YIELD: 8 to 10 slices

CITRUS CARROT RING

This attractive tube cake has the fresh tang of lemon and orange to perk up the wholesome carrot taste. It's chock-full of walnuts and raisins, giving it a most appealing heartiness.

1 cup (2 sticks) butter or margarine, softened
1 cup granulated sugar
1 cup brown sugar
4 eggs
2 tablespoons grated orange peel
1 tablespoon grated lemon peel
2 tablespoons orange juice
3 tablespoons freshly squeezed lemon juice

1 pound carrots, grated (about 4 cups)
1½ cups white flour
1½ cups whole wheat flour
2 teaspoons baking powder
1 teaspoon cinnamon
¼ teaspoon salt
1 cup coarsely chopped walnuts
1 cup raisins

1. In a large bowl, cream the butter or margarine with the sugars. Beat in the eggs, then the citrus peels and juices. Stir in the carrots.
2. In another bowl, stir together the flours, baking powder, cinnamon, and salt. Beat into the carrot mixture and then stir in the walnuts and raisins.
3. Turn the batter into a greased and floured tube pan. Bake the cake in a 350° oven for about 1½ hours, or until it tests done with a toothpick. Transfer to a rack to cool.

YIELD: 20 servings

OLD-FASHIONED GLAZED
PINEAPPLE–CARROT CAKE

This is a traditional American recipe. Carrots, crushed pineapple, walnuts, and coconut combine to make an immensely flavorful cake. After baking, the cake is topped with a glaze that penetrates it throughout to create a marvelously moist texture.

Cake Batter:

3 eggs
1½ cups sugar
½ cup salad oil
⅔ cup yogurt
2 teaspoons vanilla
2 cups flour
1 teaspoon baking soda
¼ teaspoon salt
2 teaspoons cinnamon

1 can (about 8½ ounces) crushed pineapple, preferably juice-packed, undrained
2 cups grated carrots
1 cup coarsely chopped walnuts
1 cup shredded coconut

Glaze:

⅔ cup sugar
¼ teaspoon baking soda
⅓ cup yogurt
⅓ cup (5⅓ tablespoons) butter or margarine

2 tablespoons honey
½ teaspoon vanilla

———

1. In a large bowl, beat the eggs. Gradually beat in the sugar until the mixture is thick and pale. Beat in the oil, then the yogurt and vanilla.
2. In another bowl, stir together the flour, baking soda, salt, and cinnamon. Beat into the liquid mixture. Stir in the pineapple with its juice, and the carrots, walnuts, and coconut.
3. Turn the batter into a greased and floured 9" x 13" pan. Bake the cake in a 350° oven for 45 minutes, or until it tests done with a toothpick.

4. Meanwhile, combine all glaze ingredients except the vanilla in a saucepan. Heat to the boiling point, stirring occasionally. Boil for 5 minutes. Remove from the heat and stir in the vanilla.
5. Prick the baked cake all over with a fork and pour the glaze over it. Let sit until glaze is fully absorbed. NOTE: Store the cake in the refrigerator.

YIELD: 24 servings

CARROT–BEET CAKE

In this most unusual and nutritious carrot cake, sweet beets add additional flavor and texture. Although the batter is a lovely shade of pink before baking, the cake emerges from the oven a rather tweedy brown color—still very appealing.

4 eggs
1½ cups sugar
½ cup salad oil
2 teaspoons vanilla
1 cup whole wheat flour
1 cup white flour
2 teaspoons baking soda

¼ teaspoon salt
½ cup coarsely chopped
  walnuts
2 cups shredded carrots
1 cup shredded raw peeled
  beets

———

1. In a large bowl, beat the eggs. Gradually beat in the sugar. When done, the mixture should be thick and pale. Beat in the oil and vanilla.
2. In another bowl, stir together the flours, baking soda, and salt. Beat into the liquid mixture, then stir in the walnuts, carrots, and beets.
3. Turn the batter into a greased and floured 9" x 13" baking pan. Bake the cake in a 350° oven for 40 minutes, or until it tests done with a toothpick. Transfer to a rack to cool.

YIELD: 20 servings

Cakes
With Zucchini

Zucchini, being so soft a vegetable, can be quickly shredded using the coarse blade of a hand grater. You may also use the grating blade of a food processor but not a blender, as this will turn the zucchini into pulp. Choose firm zucchini that are medium in size—huge overgrown squash are too watery and flavorless for use in baking. After grating the *unpeeled* zucchini, gently pat it with a paper towel to absorb excess moisture. Do not squeeze it dry, though, for it is the moistness of the zucchini that gives baked goods made with it their marvelous texture.

CHOCOLATE ZUCCHINI CAKE

Of all the recipes printed in my newspaper columns, this one, which appeared just when zucchini breads were coming into vogue, attracted the most attention and praise: attention because it is unusual and a conversation piece; praise because the shredded zucchini makes for a wonderfully moist chocolate cake. When the squash season is at its zenith, do try this fabulous dessert.

9 tablespoons (1 stick plus 1 tablespoon) butter or margarine, softened
2 cups sugar
3 eggs
3 1-ounce squares unsweetened chocolate, melted
2 teaspoons vanilla
2 teaspoons grated orange rind

½ cup milk
2 cups coarsely shredded zucchini
2½ cups flour
2½ teaspoons baking powder
1½ teaspoons baking soda
¼ teaspoon salt
1 teaspoon cinnamon

1. In a large bowl, cream the butter or margarine with the sugar. Beat in the eggs, then the melted chocolate, vanilla, orange rind, and milk. Stir in the zucchini.
2. In another bowl, stir together the flour, baking powder, baking soda, salt, and cinnamon. Stir into the zucchini mixture until the dry ingredients are thoroughly moistened.
3. Turn the batter into a greased and floured tube pan. Bake the cake in a 350° oven for 1 hour, or until it tests done with a toothpick. Transfer to a rack to cool.

YIELD: 16 servings

ZUCCHINI SPICE CAKE

Here's a nutritious zucchini cake that's well-flavored with orange rind and a variety of spices. The chopped bananas lend a pleasantly fruity sweetness.

3 eggs
1¼ cups brown sugar
¼ cup molasses
½ cup salad oil
1 teaspoon vanilla
1½ teaspoons lemon juice
  plus enough milk to equal
  ½ cup liquid
1 teaspoon grated orange
  rind

2 cups flour
2 teaspoons baking powder
1 teaspoon baking soda
2 teaspoons cinnamon
1 teaspoon nutmeg
¼ teaspoon salt
1½ cups shredded zucchini
1 banana, finely diced
1 cup coarsely chopped
  walnuts

1. In a large bowl, beat the eggs. Gradually beat in the brown sugar until the mixture is thick. Beat in the molasses and oil, then the lemon-milk mixture, vanilla, and orange rind.
2. In another bowl, stir together the flour, baking powder, baking soda, cinnamon, nutmeg, and salt. Beat into the liquid mixture. Stir in the zucchini, banana, and walnuts.
3. Turn the batter into a greased and floured 9" x 13" baking pan. Bake the cake in a 350° oven for 40 minutes, or until it tests done with a toothpick. Let cool on a rack.

YIELD: 15 servings

Cakes
With Pumpkin Puree

When a recipe calls for pumpkin puree, you have several options: You may purchase canned solid-pack pumpkin (not pumpkin pie filling, which contains additional ingredients). Or, since winter squash is so similar to pumpkin, you may purchase frozen cooked and mashed squash and let it thaw.

You may also make your own. *To make pumpkin or squash puree:* Cut the vegetable in half and scoop out the seeds. Place, cut side down, on a baking sheet and add ½ to 1 inch of water. Bake the vegetable in a 350° oven until it is tender (about 50 minutes for acorn squash, 1½ hours for a medium-sized pumpkin). Scoop out the pulp and puree it with a ricer or in a blender or food processor. Cooked, pureed squash or pumpkin may be frozen in small plastic containers and thawed before using.

PUMPKIN CHOCOLATE CHIP CAKE

Here's a dramatic tube cake that never fails to draw oohs and aahs of praise from everyone. Moist with pumpkin, dark with spices, and chock-full of nuts, raisins, and chocolate chips, this is truly a cake for festive occasions (but if there's no special event coming up, don't hesitate to whip it up for yourself).

4 eggs
2 cups sugar
1 cup (2 sticks) butter or
  margarine, melted
2 cups cooked pumpkin
  puree (homemade or
  canned solid-pack
  pumpkin; *not* pumpkin
  pie mix)
1 cup white flour
1 cup whole wheat flour
2 teaspoons baking powder
1 teaspoon baking soda

¼ teaspoon salt
1½ teaspoons cinnamon
½ teaspoon ground cloves
¼ teaspoon nutmeg
¼ teaspoon ginger
2 cups bran cereal, such as
  All-Bran
1 6-ounce package semi-
  sweet chocolate morsels
⅔ cup coarsely chopped
  walnuts
⅔ cup raisins

1. In a large bowl, beat the eggs. Gradually beat in the sugar until the mixture is thick and pale. Beat in the melted butter or margarine and then the pumpkin.
2. In another bowl, stir together the flours, baking powder, baking soda, salt, spices, and bran. Beat into the pumpkin mixture. Stir in the chocolate, nuts, and raisins.
3. Turn the batter into a greased and floured tube pan. Bake the cake in a 350° oven for 1 hour and 10 minutes, or until it tests done with a toothpick. Transfer to a rack to cool.

YIELD: 16 servings

PUMPKIN–PRUNE CAKE

This small, spicy cake is remarkably quick and easy to put together—and also great served warm from the oven. The prunes nicely complement the pumpkin both in flavor and in color. NOTE: Dried prunes come in two forms—very firm and dried, and moist-packed. This latter form, usually labeled "ready to eat," is preferable in the recipe.

⅓ cup (5⅓ tablespoons) butter or margarine, softened
¾ cup sugar
1 egg
½ cup cooked pumpkin puree, (homemade or canned solid-pack pumpkin; *not* pumpkin pie mix)

⅓ cup milk
1 cup plus 3 tablespoons flour
2 teaspoons baking powder
¼ teaspoon salt
½ teaspoon ginger
1 teaspoon cinnamon
½ cup chopped moist prunes

1. In a bowl, cream the butter or margarine with the sugar. Beat in the egg, then the pumpkin puree and milk.
2. In another bowl, stir together the flour, baking powder, salt, and spices. Beat into the pumpkin mixture and then stir in the prunes.
3. Turn the cake into a greased and floured 8" x 8" baking pan. Bake the cake in a 375° oven for 35 minutes, or until it tests done with a toothpick. Transfer to a rack to cool.

YIELD: 9 servings

FESTIVE PUMPKIN CAKE

Here's a fine finish to your next Thanksgiving feast. A delightful pumpkin spice cake is adorned with colorful apricots and crimson cranberries in an arrangement that's as pretty as the autumn leaves. The cake is prepared as you would an upside-down cake—use a deep 9" or 10" skillet with an ovenproof handle.

Topping:
20 dried apricot halves
boiling water
4 tablespoons butter or
   margarine

½ cup brown sugar
¾ cup whole-berry cran-
   berry sauce, homemade
   or canned

Cake Batter:
2 eggs
1¼ cups granulated sugar
½ cup (1 stick) butter or
   margarine, melted
1 cup cooked pumpkin
   puree, homemade or
   canned solid-pack
   pumpkin; *not* pumpkin
   pie mix

¼ cup water
1 cup white flour
¾ cup whole wheat flour
¼ teaspoon salt
1 teaspoon baking soda
½ teaspoon cinnamon
¼ teaspoon nutmeg
½ cup coarsely chopped
   walnuts

---

1. Pour boiling water over the apricots (just enough to cover). Let sit 5 minutes, and then drain well.
2. Meanwhile, melt the 4 tablespoons butter or margarine in a deep 9" or 10" skillet with an ovenproof handle. Remove from the heat, stir in the brown sugar, and spread to coat bottom of pan evenly. Arrange the apricots on the bottom and fill in the spaces between them with small spoonfuls of cranberry sauce.
3. In a large bowl, beat the eggs. Gradually beat in the granulated sugar until the mixture is thick. Beat in the melted butter or margarine, then the pumpkin and water.

4. In another bowl, stir together the flours, salt, baking soda, and spices. Beat into the pumpkin mixture and then stir in the walnuts.
5. Gently pour the batter into the prepared pan. Bake the cake in a 350° oven for 1 hour, or until it tests done with a toothpick. Run a knife around the edge and immediately tip upside down onto an ovenproof plate. Bake the cake 5 minutes longer to set the topping. NOTE: Since the topping on this cake is quite moist, the cake should be stored in the refrigerator.

YIELD: 12 servings

Cakes
With Other Vegetables

FRESH YAM CAKE

This is similar to the popular carrot cake, but the yams lend a sweeter flavor. It's a hearty, moist cake that's great warm from the oven with a scoop of vanilla ice cream. A fine fall family dessert.

4 eggs
1½ cups sugar
1 cup (2 sticks) butter or
  margarine, melted
¼ cup water
1¼ cups white flour
1 cup whole wheat flour
1 tablespoon baking powder

2 teaspoons cinnamon
1 teaspoon ginger
½ teaspoon ground cloves
¼ teaspoon salt
1½ cups grated raw peeled
  yams (or sweet potatoes)
½ cup coarsely chopped
  walnuts

1. In a large bowl, beat the eggs. Gradually beat in the sugar until the mixture is thick and pale. Beat in the melted butter or margarine, then the water.
2. In another bowl, stir together the flours, spices, and salt. Beat into the liquid mixture and then stir in the grated yams and walnuts.
3. Turn the batter into a greased and floured 9" x 13" baking pan. Bake the cake in a 350° oven for 45 minutes, or until it tests done with a toothpick. Let cool on a rack.

YIELD: 20 servings

CHOCOLATE SAUERKRAUT CAKE

This cake is included here because it is such an oddity in the annals of cake baking. Although it sounds most unappetizing, the sauerkraut flavor all but disappears when the cake is baked. What does remain, however (as in most vegetable cakes), is an especially moist and tender texture. Like the Chocolate Zucchini Cake, this is definitely a conversation piece.

⅓ cup (5⅓ tablespoons) butter or margarine, softened
1 cup sugar
2 eggs
2 1-ounce squares unsweetened chocolate, melted

⅔ cup water
1 teaspoon vanilla
1½ cups flour
¾ teaspoon baking soda
1 teaspoon baking powder
¼ teaspoon salt
½ cup well-drained canned sauerkraut, chopped

1. In a bowl, cream the butter or margarine with the sugar. Beat in the eggs, then the melted chocolate, water, and vanilla.
2. In another bowl, stir together the flour, baking soda, baking powder, and salt. Beat into the creamed mixture and then stir in the sauerkraut.
3. Turn the batter into a greased and floured 8" x 8" pan. Bake the cake in a 350° oven for 35 minutes, or until it tests done with a toothpick. Transfer to a rack to cool.

YIELD: 9 servings

Chocolate Cakes

Chocolate cakes hardly need any introduction. In some people's minds, cakes almost by definition are always chocolate, so fond are they of this flavor. And even for those less addicted to this absolutely marvelous substance, chocolate cakes remain among their favorites.

In this chapter, you'll find plenty of deep, dark chocolate cakes, all of which can be quickly prepared to satisfy any chocoholic's cravings. Choose from among beautiful marble cakes, chocolate upside-down cakes, and just plain great-eating chocolatey chocolate cakes.

DARK CHOCOLATE ORANGE CAKE

This cake has the texture of crumbly, cakelike brownies. It's dry and grainy, with a very dark chocolate flavor that's not too sweet and contains a hint of orange perfume.

10 tablespoons (1 stick plus
  2 tablespoons) butter,
  softened (use real butter,
  if possible)
1½ cups sugar
4 eggs
⅔ cup sour cream
1 teaspoon vanilla

grated rind of 1 orange
2 cups flour
⅔ cup cocoa, sifted if lumpy
¼ teaspoon baking soda
¼ teaspoon salt
½ cup coarsely chopped
  almonds

1. In a bowl, cream the butter with the sugar. Beat in the eggs, then the sour cream, vanilla, and orange rind.
2. In another bowl, stir together the flour, cocoa, baking soda, and salt. Beat into the creamed mixture just until incorporated and then stir in the almonds.
3. Turn the batter into a greased and floured tube pan. Bake in a 350° oven for 1 hour, or until it tests done with a toothpick. Let cool on a rack.

YIELD: 16 servings

RICHEST-*EVER* CHOCOLATE POUND CAKE

Dense, dark, delicious, and delectable are only a few of the adjectives used to describe this rich, rich pound cake. A must for chocolate fans!

4 eggs, separated
1 cup (2 sticks) butter or margarine, softened (use at least half real butter, if possible)
2 cups sugar
1 6-ounce package semisweet chocolate morsels, melted in ½ cup water

1 cup buttermilk, or use 1 tablespoon lemon juice plus enough nonfat or skimmed milk to equal 1 cup liquid
1 teaspoon vanilla
2½ cups flour
1 teaspoon baking soda
¼ teaspoon salt

1. Beat the egg whites until stiff, and set aside.
2. In a large bowl, cream the butter with the sugar (you need not wash the beaters between steps). Beat in the egg yolks, then the melted chocolate, buttermilk, and vanilla.
3. In a bowl, stir together the flour, baking soda, and salt. Beat into the chocolate mixture. Stir in about one-third of the egg whites to lighten the batter and then fold in the rest gently but thoroughly.
4. Turn the batter into a greased and floured tube pan. Bake in a 350° oven for 1 hour, or until the cake tests done with a toothpick. Let cool on a rack.

YIELD: 16 servings

MISSISSIPPI MUD CAKE

*Here's a popular Southern cake that's as dark and myste-
rious as the mud at the bottom of the Mississippi (but, of
course, tastes decidedly superior). This is a large attractive
tube cake that will be welcomed at any gathering, especially
one with men around.*

1¾ cups strong coffee	2 eggs
¼ cup dark rum	2 cups sugar
5 1-ounce squares	1 teaspoon vanilla
unsweetened chocolate	2 cups flour
1 cup (2 sticks) butter or	1 teaspoon baking soda
margarine	⅛ teaspoon salt

1. Place coffee and rum in a saucepan and heat to a simmer.
   Add the chocolate and butter or margarine. Cook, stirring,
   occasionally, until both are melted. Remove from the heat.
2. In a large bowl, beat the eggs. Gradually beat in the sugar
   until the mixture is thick. Beat in the vanilla and the
   chocolate mixture.
3. In another bowl, stir together the flour, baking soda, and
   salt. Beat into the chocolate mixture.
4. Turn the batter into a greased and floured tube pan. Bake
   in a 275° oven for 1½ hours, or until the cake tests done
   with a toothpick. Transfer to a rack to cool.

YIELD: 16 servings

CALIFORNIA FUDGE CAKE

Cupfuls of pecans and dates give this dark fudge cake a definite California flavor. It's easy to whip up and feeds a crowd. For a party, you might top each square with a scoop of ice cream.

¾ cup (1½ stick) butter or margarine, softened
2½ cups sugar
6 eggs
6 ounces unsweetened chocolate, melted
1½ teaspoons vanilla
1 cup milk

3 cups flour
1 tablespoon baking powder
¼ teaspoon salt
3 cups chopped dates, tossed with 1½ tablespoons flour
2½ cups coarsely chopped pecans

1. In a very large bowl, cream the butter with the sugar. Beat in the eggs, then the chocolate and vanilla. Beat in the milk.
2. In another bowl, stir together the flour, baking powder, and salt. Beat into the chocolate mixture and then stir in the dates and pecans.
3. Turn the batter into a greased and floured 9" x 13" baking pan. Bake the cake in a 350° oven for about 1 hour and 20 minutes, or until it tests done with a toothpick. Transfer to a rack to cool.

YIELD: 24 servings

CHOCOLATE SOUR CREAM CAKE

Dates add richness to this already ultrarich chocolate sour cream cake. The cake is flat and dense, with a wonderful brownie-like quality.

10 ounces pitted dates, finely chopped
½ cup boiling water
½ teaspoon baking soda
1 cup (2 sticks) butter or margarine, softened
1⅓ cups sugar
2 eggs
⅔ cup sour cream
1 teaspoon vanilla

2 1-ounce squares unsweetened chocolate, melted
2 1-ounce squares (or use ⅓ cup morsels) semisweet chocolate, melted
1½ cups flour
¼ teaspoon salt
1 cup coarsely chopped walnuts

---

1. In a small bowl, pour the boiling water over the dates. Stir in the baking soda and let sit while preparing the batter.
2. In another bowl, cream the butter or margarine with the sugar. Beat in the eggs, then the sour cream, vanilla, and melted chocolate (these two chocolates may be melted in the same saucepan).
3. In a small bowl, stir together the flour and salt. Beat into the chocolate mixture. Stir in the walnuts and the dates, along with any liquid in the bowl.
4. Spread the batter evenly in a greased and floured 9" x 13" baking pan. Bake the cake in a 350° oven for 45 minutes, or until it tests done with a toothpick. Transfer to a rack to cool.

YIELD: 20 servings

DOUBLE CHOCOLATE MARBLE CAKE

A dark swirl of cocoa enhances this rich, fudgy chocolate cake. Because the egg whites are beaten separately, there's a bit more work involved in making this cake than in some others; but the wonderful texture that results is certainly worth the added effort.

Cake Batter:

6 eggs, separated	1 teaspoon vanilla
1 cup (2 sticks) butter, softened (use real butter, if possible)	1 cup sour cream
	2½ cups flour
	½ cup cocoa, sifted if lumpy
1 cup granulated sugar	¼ teaspoon salt
1 cup brown sugar	1 teaspoon baking soda

Marbling Mixture: (Mix ingredients together)
⅓ cup cocoa, sifted if lumpy   ½ cup granulated sugar

---

1. In a large bowl, beat the egg whites until stiff, and set aside.
2. In another large bowl, cream the butter with the sugars. Beat in the egg yolks, then the vanilla and sour cream.
3. In another bowl, stir together the flour, cocoa, salt, and baking soda. Beat into the creamed mixture. Stir about one-third of the egg whites into the batter to lighten it and then fold in the rest gently but thoroughly.
4. Spread about one-fourth of the batter into a greased and floured tube pan and sprinkle with about one-third of the cocoa-sugar mixture. Continue repeating layers, ending with the batter. With a knife, lightly swirl the batter and cocoa mixture together.
5. Bake the cake in a 325° oven for 1¾ hours, or until it tests done with a toothpick. Let cool on a rack.

YIELD: 16 to 20 servings

HONEYED CHOCOLATE UPSIDE-DOWN CAKE

Brown sugar, honey, and nuts are spread on the bottom of the baking pan before adding the chocolate batter. When done, the cake is tipped upside down, and the topping forms an attractive, crunchy glaze. The cake tastes especially moist and fudgy served warm from the oven.

Topping:

2 tablespoons butter or
    margarine, softened
2 tablespoons brown sugar

⅓ cup honey
½ cup finely chopped
    walnuts

Cake Batter:

5 tablespoons butter or
    margarine, softened
⅔ cup granulated sugar
1 egg
1 teaspoon vanilla

¾ cup milk
1 cup flour
⅓ cup cocoa, sifted if lumpy
1 teaspoon baking powder
¼ teaspoon salt

1. Mix together the butter or margarine, brown sugar, and honey. Spread over the bottom of a well-greased (but not floured) 8" x 8" pan. Sprinkle with the walnuts.
2. In a bowl, cream together the butter or margarine with the granulated sugar. Beat in the egg, then the vanilla and milk.
3. In another bowl, stir together the flour, cocoa, baking powder, and salt. Beat into the creamed ingredients.
4. Turn the batter carefully into the prepared pan. Bake the cake in a 350° oven for 30 minutes, or until it tests done with a toothpick. Run a knife around the edge of the cake and tip the cake upside down onto an ovenproof plate. Bake the cake 5 minutes longer; this will serve to make the top less moist.

YIELD: 9 servings

CHOCOLATE "PLUM PUDDING" CAKE

Somehow the richness of the chocolate, moistness of the applesauce, and fruitiness of the raisins all combine to produce a taste and texture remarkably like traditional Christmas plum pudding—with far less effort! This festive cake is best served chilled, with a dollop of brandy-flavored whipped cream on the side.

⅔ cup raisins, soaked in boiling water to cover for 5 minutes and then drained

¾ cup (1½ sticks) butter or margarine, softened

1½ cups sugar

3 eggs

2 cups homemade or store-bought applesauce, sweetened or unsweetened

¾ cup white flour

¾ cup whole wheat flour

2 teaspoons baking soda

¼ teaspoon salt

1 tablespoon cinnamon

½ teaspoon nutmeg

⅓ cup cocoa, sifted if lumpy

½ cup coarsely chopped walnuts

---

1. In a large bowl, cream the butter or margarine with the sugar. Beat in the eggs, then the applesauce.
2. In another bowl, stir together the flours, baking soda, salt, spices, and cocoa. Beat into the applesauce mixture and then stir in the raisins and walnuts.
3. Turn the batter into a greased and floured tube pan. Bake the cake in a 350° oven for 1 hour and 20 minutes, or until it tests done with a toothpick. Let cool on a rack and then chill.

YIELD: 12 servings

CHOCOLATE APPLESAUCE CAKE

Moist with applesauce and full of raisins and pecans, this is a chocolate cake to win over any chocolate fan. Dark rum in the batter and sprinkled over the baked cake adds an exotic touch. Since this cake calls for no eggs, it has an especially dense texture (and also requires one less step in the preparation).

½ cup (1 stick) butter or
    margarine, softened
1¼ cups sugar
½ cup milk
1½ cups homemade or
    store-bought applesauce,
    sweetened or unsweetened
2 tablespoons plus ¼ cup
    dark rum, divided usage

2 cups flour
¼ cup cocoa, sifted if lumpy
2 teaspoons baking soda
1 teaspoon cinnamon
1 teaspoon nutmeg
⅛ teaspoon salt
1 cup raisins
1 cup coarsely chopped
    pecans

1. In a bowl, cream the butter or margarine with the sugar. Beat in the milk, applesauce, and 2 tablespoons rum.
2. In another bowl, stir together the flour, cocoa, baking soda, spices, and salt. Beat into the creamed mixture and then stir in the raisins and pecans.
3. Turn the batter into a greased and floured 9" x 13" baking pan. Bake the cake in a 350° oven for 45 minutes, or until it tests done with a toothpick. Immediately after removing the cake from the oven, sprinkle it with the remaining ¼ cup rum. Let cool on a rack. This cake improves if allowed to sit for a day or so before eating.

YIELD: 20 servings

CHOCOLATE BANANA CAKE

This supermoist chocolate cake is rich with the fruity taste of banana. In this and all other banana cakes, be certain to use fully ripe bananas—the darker the skin, the sweeter and more flavorful the cake.

9 tablespoons (1 stick plus
  1 tablespoon) butter or
  margarine, softened
1¼ cups sugar
2 eggs
1½ teaspoons lemon juice
  plus enough milk to equal
  ½ cup liquid

1 cup bananas, mashed
1 cup flour
½ cup cocoa, sifted if lumpy
¼ teaspoon salt
1 teaspoon baking soda

---

1. In a bowl, cream the butter or margarine with the sugar. Beat in the eggs, then the lemon-milk mixture and the bananas.
2. In another bowl, stir together the flour, cocoa, salt, and baking soda. Beat into the banana mixture.
3. Turn the batter into a greased and floured 8" x 10" baking pan. Bake the cake in a 350° oven for 35 minutes, or until it tests done with a toothpick. Transfer to a rack to cool.

YIELD: 10 servings

CHOCOLATE CHERRY RING

This cake is like those lovely cherry-filled chocolate bon bons. Each slice contains plenty of juicy dark cherries, surrounded by a chocolate-flecked, spicy batter. A scoop of cherry-vanilla ice cream would top each slice of cake superbly.

3 eggs
½ cup granulated sugar
½ cup brown sugar
½ cup (1 stick) butter or
   margarine, melted
½ cup orange juice
½ teaspoon vanilla
2 cups flour
¼ teaspoon baking soda
1½ teaspoons baking
   powder

½ teaspoon cinnamon
¼ teaspoon nutmeg
¼ teaspoon salt
3 ounces (½ cup) semisweet
   chocolate morsels, finely
   grated
1 cup finely chopped
   walnuts
1 16-ounce can well-drained
   pitted dark, sweet cherries

1. In a large bowl, beat the eggs. Gradually beat in the granulated sugar and then the brown sugar. When done, the mixture should be thick. Beat in the melted butter or margarine, then the orange juice and vanilla.
2. In another bowl, stir together the flour, baking soda, baking powder, spices, and salt. Beat into the liquid mixture. Stir in the chocolate, walnuts, and cherries.
3. Turn the batter into a greased and floured tube pan. Bake the cake in a 325° oven for 45 minutes, or until it tests done with a toothpick. Transfer to a rack to cool.

YIELD: 12 to 14 servings

CHOCOLATE MARASCHINO CAKE

Here's a cake that's a great favorite among children, who are always fond of maraschino cherries. The cake is quite sweet and very chocolatey. It would make a fine choice for any youngster's birthday party. A blender or food processor makes preparing the batter a breeze, for either machine finely chops the cherries in no time. But, if you don't own one of these appliances, you can mince the cherries by hand.

½ cup (1 stick) butter or margarine, softened
1 cup sugar
1 egg
1 8-ounce bottle maraschino cherries, stemmed and drained (reserve liquid)
2 1-ounce squares unsweetened chocolate, melted

1 tablespoon lemon juice plus enough milk to equal 1 cup liquid
1 teaspoon vanilla
2 cups flour
1 teaspoon baking soda
¼ teaspoon salt

To Prepare the Batter in Blender or Food Processor:

1. Place the butter or margarine, sugar, egg, cherry juice, melted chocolate, lemon-milk mixture, and vanilla in the blender or food processor. Process until smooth. Add the cherries and process until finely chopped.
2. In a large bowl, stir together the flour, baking soda, and salt. Add the liquid ingredients and stir to mix well.

To Prepare the Batter in a Mixing Bowl:

1. In a large bowl, cream the butter or margarine with the sugar. Beat in the egg, then the cherry juice, melted chocolate, lemon-milk mixture, and vanilla.
2. In another bowl, stir together the flour, baking soda, and salt. Beat into the creamed mixture. Finely chop the cherries and stir them into the batter.

To Bake:

3. Turn the batter into a greased and floured 9" x 13" baking pan. Bake the cake in a 350° oven for 40 minutes, or until it tests done with a toothpick. Transfer to a rack to cool.
YIELD: 18 servings

CHOCOLATE MOLASSES CAKE

Molasses makes chocolate cake even darker, moister, and more satisfying than usual. If you want a special treat, serve it warm or cooled with vanilla ice cream.

¾ cup (1½ sticks) butter or margarine, softened
⅔ cup sugar
2 eggs
⅔ cup molasses
1 teaspoon vanilla
1 teaspoon lemon juice plus enough milk to equal ¾ cup liquid

1½ cups flour
½ cup cocoa, sifted if lumpy
1 teaspoon baking soda
¼ teaspoon salt

1. In a large bowl, cream the butter or margarine with the sugar. Beat in the eggs, then the molasses, vanilla, and lemon-milk mixture.
2. In another bowl, stir together the flour, cocoa, baking soda, and salt. Beat into the creamed mixture.
3. Turn the batter into a greased and floured 8" x 10" baking pan. Bake the cake in a 375° oven for 25 minutes, or until it tests done with a toothpick. Let cool on a rack.
YIELD: 10 servings

POTATO FUDGE CAKE

Potatoes add a rich, moist quality to the texture of the cake, while affecting its wonderful fudgy flavor not at all. Spices and grated lemon rind add an elusive taste to this attractive and eminently appealing tube cake.

4 eggs, separated
1 cup (2 sticks) butter or
   margarine, softened
2 cups sugar
3 1-ounce squares unsweetened chocolate, melted
½ cup milk
grated rind of 1 lemon
2½ cups flour

1 tablespoon baking powder
¼ teaspoon salt
½ teaspoon nutmeg
½ teaspoon cinnamon
½ teaspoon ground cloves
1 cup grated peeled raw
   potatoes
½ cup coarsely chopped
   walnuts

1. In a bowl, beat the egg whites until stiff, and set aside.
2. In a large bowl, cream the butter with the sugar (you need not clean the beaters between steps). Beat in the egg yolks, then the chocolate, milk, and lemon rind.
3. In another bowl, stir together the flour, baking powder, salt, and spices. Beat into the chocolate mixture. Stir in the potatoes and walnuts. Fold in about one-third of the egg whites to lighten the batter and then fold in the rest gently but thoroughly.
4. Turn the batter into a greased and floured tube pan. Bake the cake in a 325° oven for 1¼ hours, or until it tests done with a toothpick. Transfer to a rack to cool.

YIELD: 12 to 14 servings

CHOCOLATE POPPY SEED CAKE

The subtle nutty flavor of poppy seeds enhances this ultra-rich chocolate cake that contains no flour. It's very dense, very moist, and altogether delightful—especially when served with a dollop of whipped cream.

6 eggs, separated
⅛ teaspoon cream of tartar
11 tablespoons (1 stick plus
   3 tablespoons) butter or
   margarine, softened
¾ cup sugar

6 ounces semisweet
   chocolate morsels, melted
¾ cup poppy seeds
2 tablespoons fine, dry,
   unseasoned bread crumbs

1. In a large bowl, beat the egg whites with the cream of tartar until stiff peaks form. Set aside.
2. In another bowl, cream the butter or margarine with the sugar (there is no need to clean the beaters between these steps). Beat in the egg yolks. Then beat in the melted chocolate, poppy seeds, and bread crumbs.
3. Stir about one-third of the egg whites into the batter to lighten it. Then fold in the rest gently but thoroughly.
4. Turn the batter into a greased and floured tube pan. Bake in a 350° oven for 50 minutes, or until the cake tests clean with a toothpick. Let cool on a rack.

YIELD: 10 servings

CHOCOLATE PEANUT BUTTER CAKE

Anyone who's addicted to those lovely chocolate peanut butter candy cups is certain to equally enjoy a slice of this special dark cake.

10 tablespoons (1 stick plus
  2 tablespoons) butter or
  margarine, softened
½ cup peanut butter,
  preferably chunk style
1¾ cups sugar
2 eggs
1 teaspoon vanilla

1 cup water
1 cup white flour
1 cup whole wheat flour
6 tablespoons cocoa, sifted
  if lumpy
1 teaspoon baking soda
¼ teaspoon salt

1. In a large bowl, cream together the butter and peanut butter with the sugar. Beat in the eggs, then the vanilla and water.
2. In another bowl, stir together the flours, cocoa, baking soda, and salt. Beat these dry ingredients into the creamed mixture.
3. Turn the batter into a greased and floured tube pan. Bake in a 350° oven for 1 hour, or until the cake tests done with a toothpick. Let cool on a rack.

YIELD: 12 servings

CHOCOLATE SYRUP CAKE

Most chocolate and white marble cakes instruct the baker to flavor half the batter with a chocolate mixture and then layer the two different batters in the pan. For this cake, however, a rich chocolate syrup is poured over the white batter; it seeps in gently, making lovely chocolate indentations throughout the cake.

Chocolate Syrup

5 tablespoons butter or margarine	½ cup water
3 tablespoons cocoa, sifted if lumpy	⅔ cup sugar
	1 teaspoon vanilla
	⅓ cup finely chopped pecans

Cake Batter:

4 tablespoons (½ stick) butter or margarine, softened	½ cup milk
	1 teaspoon vanilla
¾ cup sugar	1½ cups flour
1 egg	1 teaspoon baking powder
	¼ teaspoon salt

1. Make the syrup: Melt the butter in a small saucepan. Add the cocoa, water, and sugar. Bring to a boil, stirring constantly. Remove from the heat and stir in the vanilla. Let cool while preparing the cake batter.
2. In a bowl, cream the butter or margarine with the sugar. Beat in the egg, then the milk and vanilla.
3. In another bowl, stir together the flour, baking powder, and salt. Beat into the creamed mixture.
4. Turn the batter into a greased and floured 8" x 8" pan. Pour the chocolate syrup gently over the batter and sprinkle with the pecans. Bake the cake in a 350° oven for 40 minutes, or until it tests done with a toothpick. Transfer to a rack to cool. NOTE: Since this cake is so moist, it should be stored in the refrigerator.

YIELD: 8 servings

BITTERSWEET CHOCOLATE MARBLE CAKE

Here's another differently-prepared marble cake—this one with a bittersweet chocolate mixture swirled into the pound-cake-like batter. The whole wheat flour and brown sugar contribute heartiness to this unique and attractive tube cake.

Cake Batter:

6 eggs, separated	1 cup whole wheat flour
1½ cups brown sugar	1¼ cups white flour
½ cup oil	2½ teaspoons baking powder
½ cup water	¼ teaspoon salt
2 teaspoons vanilla	

Marbling Mixture (Stir all ingredients together until smooth):

¾ cup brown sugar	6 tablespoons cocoa
1 teaspoon vanilla	½ cup boiling water

1. In a bowl, beat the egg whites until stiff. Set aside.
2. In a large bowl, beat the egg yolks. Gradually beat in the brown sugar. When done, the mixture should be thick. Beat in the oil, then the water and vanilla.
3. In another bowl, stir together the flours, baking powder, and salt. Beat into the liquid mixture. Stir in one-third of the egg whites to lighten the batter and then fold in the rest gently but thoroughly.
4. Turn the batter into a greased and floured tube pan. Pour the marbling mixture over the batter and swirl gently with a knife.
5. Bake the cake in a 325° oven for 30 minutes. Raise the heat to 350° and bake 20 minutes more, or until it tests done with a toothpick. Transfer to a rack to cool.

YIELD: 16 servings

MOCHA NUT DEVIL'S FOOD CAKE

A mocha-walnut mixture forms the filling and topping of this tender, moist devil's food cake. Serve each portion warm or cooled with a scoop of vanilla ice cream and hot fudge sauce, if desired.

Cake Batter:
13⅓ tablespoons (1⅓ sticks)
   butter or margarine,
   softened
1¾ cups sugar
3 eggs
2 teaspoons lemon juice
   plus enough milk to equal
   ¾ cup liquid

½ cup water
2¼ cups flour
½ cup cocoa, sifted if lumpy
1 teaspoon baking soda
¼ teaspoon salt

Mocha Mixture: (Mix all ingredients together)
3 ounces (½ cup) semisweet
   chocolate morsels, melted
⅓ cup strong coffee

2 cups finely chopped
   walnuts

1. In a large bowl, cream the butter or margarine with the sugar. Beat in the eggs, then the lemon-milk mixture and water.
2. In another bowl, stir together the flour, cocoa, baking soda, and salt. Beat into the creamed mixture.
3. Spread half the batter in an 8" x 10" baking pan that's been greased and floured. Sprinkle with half the mocha-nut mixture and then spread with the remaining batter. Bake the cake in a 350° oven for 40 minutes, or until a toothpick inserted in it comes out clean. Immediately spread with the remaining mocha mixture and then bake 5 minutes longer. Transfer to a rack to cool.

YIELD: 12 to 14 servings

CHOCOLATE ORANGE MARBLE CAKE

In a listing of the two most compatible flavor combinations in the world, chocolate and orange would certainly rank high. Here, these two pair up in an attractive and especially moist cake.

1 cup (2 sticks) butter, softened (use at least half real butter, if possible)
1¼ cups sugar, divided usage
3 eggs
2 teaspoons vanilla
1 cup yogurt
1¾ cups flour
¾ teaspoon baking soda
¾ teaspoon baking powder
¼ teaspoon salt
grated rind of 1 orange
2 1-ounce squares unsweetened chocolate, melted
2 tablespoons orange liqueur, such as Grand Marnier, plus enough orange juice to equal ½ cup liquid

1. In a large bowl, cream the butter with 1 cup sugar. Beat in the eggs, then the vanilla and yogurt.
2. In another bowl, stir together the flour, baking soda, baking powder, and salt. Beat into the creamed ingredients.
3. Turn half of the batter into another bowl. Add the orange rind to one bowl and the melted chocolate to the other. Alternately spoon the orange and chocolate batters into a greased and floured tube pan. Swirl through the two batters with a knife to create a marbled effect.
4. Bake the cake in a 350° oven for 50 minutes, or until it tests done with a toothpick. As soon as it comes from the oven, stir together the remaining ¼ cup sugar with the liqueur-orange juice mixture, and pour this over the hot cake. Let the cake cool on a rack.

YIELD: 10 to 12 servings

Chocolate Chip Cakes

Chocolate chip cakes deserve a chapter of their own. They're for people who enjoy the taste of chocolate so much, the whole bits of candy scattered throughout the batter simply make for an even more fabulous dessert.

Just as there are endless versions of chocolate chip cookies, so, too, can the cakes vary. The batter may be dark or light. The chocolate itself may be semisweet, or milk, or even chopped-up candy bars. Sometimes the candy flecks the entire cake, or it may be sprinkled on just the top for a most attractive effect. You'll also find fruit-flavored versions, such as Banana Chocolate Chip, in other chapters of the book.

Each chocolate chip cake is unique. For fans of this type of cake—and they are legion among all age groups—each recipe is well worth trying.

FUDGE CHIP CAKE

Sour cream and brown sugar combine to make a most fudgy chocolate cake, and the chocolate chips scattered throughout add to its universal appeal. Serve it topped with a scoop of vanilla ice cream and you'll have everyone asking for seconds.

½ cup (1 stick) butter,
  softened (use real butter,
  if possible)
1½ cups brown sugar
3 eggs
4 squares unsweetened
  chocolate, melted
1½ cups sour cream
2 teaspoons vanilla
2 cups flour

2 teaspoons baking powder
½ teaspoon baking soda
⅛ teaspoon salt
1 6-ounce package
  semisweet chocolate
  chips, chopped slightly
  in the blender or food
  processor (or purchase
  mini chocolate chips)

1. In a large bowl, cream the butter with the brown sugar. Beat in the eggs, then the chocolate, sour cream, and vanilla.
2. In another bowl, stir together the flour, baking powder, baking soda, and salt. Beat into the chocolate mixture just until moistened. Stir in the chocolate chips.
3. Turn the batter into a greased and floured tube pan. Bake the cake in a 350° oven for 1¼ hours, or until it tests done with a toothpick. Let cool on a rack.

YIELD: 16 servings

DOUBLE CHOCOLATE CAKE

Here's another extra chocolaty chocolate cake for chocoholics. Just before baking, the rich chocolate batter is topped with dark chocolate candy. You may use any type of bittersweet chocolate that suits your fancy—I have used the readily available German's Sweet Chocolate in the recipe. You will need a heavy, deep 9" or 10" skillet with an ovenproof handle and a tight-fitting cover for baking the cake. If you lack one, you may substitute a dutch oven. This cake is especially delicious warm but may also be served at room temperature.

½ cup (1 stick) butter or margarine, softened
1¼ cups brown sugar
3 eggs
1½ teaspoons lemon juice plus enough milk to equal ½ cup liquid
1 teaspoon vanilla

½ cup water
1½ cups flour
½ cup cocoa, sifted if lumpy
1 teaspoon baking soda
¼ teaspoon salt
3 ounces dark chocolate, finely grated

1. In a large bowl, cream the butter or margarine with the brown sugar. Beat in the eggs, then the lemon-milk mixture, vanilla, and water.
2. In another bowl, stir together the flour, cocoa, baking soda, and salt. Beat into the creamed ingredients.
3. Turn the batter into a greased and floured 9" or 10" skillet with an ovenproof handle and sprinkle with the grated chocolate. Cover the pan and bake the cake in a 350° oven for about 50 minutes, or until it tests done with a toothpick.

YIELD: 8 to 10 servings

CHOCOLATE ALMOND POUND CAKE

Crushed milk chocolate bars and almonds add the flavor of America's favorite candy to this magnificently tall pound cake.

6 eggs, separated
1 cup (2 sticks) butter or
   margarine, softened
2 cups sugar
2 teaspoons vanilla
1 tablespoon vinegar plus
   enough milk to equal 1
   cup liquid
3 cups flour
1 teaspoon baking powder

½ teaspoon baking soda
½ teaspoon nutmeg
¼ teaspoon salt
10 ounces milk chocolate,
   coarsely crushed in the
   blender or food processor
   (or hand chop with a
   knife, if necessary)
¼ cup finely chopped
   almonds

1. In a bowl, beat the egg whites until stiff, and set aside.
2. In a large bowl, cream the butter or margarine with the sugar. Beat in the egg yolks, then the vanilla and vinegar-milk mixture.

3. In another bowl, stir together the flour, baking soda, baking powder, nutmeg, and salt. Beat into the creamed mixture.
4. Stir in the chocolate, almonds, and one-third of the beaten egg whites. Fold in the rest of the egg whites gently but thoroughly.
5. Turn the batter into a greased and floured tube pan. Bake the cake in a 350° oven for about 1 hour and 50 minutes, or until it tests done with a toothpick. Let cool on a rack before removing from pan.

YIELD: 20 servings

CHOCOLATE CRUNCH-TOPPED CAKE

Some of the semisweet chocolate goes into the cake batter, while the rest is mixed with graham cracker crumbs and nuts to form a delightful, crunchy topping that kids, especially, will go for.

Cake Batter:

½ cup (1 stick) butter or margarine, softened

1½ cups sugar

2 eggs

1 teaspoon vanilla

⅓ 6-ounce package semisweet chocolate morsels, melted

4 teaspoons lemon juice plus enough milk to equal 1¼ cups liquid

1 cup white flour

1 cup whole wheat flour

1 teaspoon baking soda

¼ teaspoon salt

Topping: (Mix all ingredients together until crumbly)

⅔ 6-ounce package semisweet chocolate morsels

½ cup coarsely crushed graham cracker crumbs

⅓ cup (5⅓ tablespoons) butter or margarine, melted

½ cup chopped walnuts

1. In a large bowl, cream the butter or margarine with the sugar. Beat in the eggs, then the vanilla, melted chocolate, and lemon-milk mixture.
2. In another bowl, stir together the flours, baking soda, and salt. Beat into the creamed mixture.
3. Spread the batter evenly in a greased and floured 9" x 13" baking pan. Sprinkle with the topping mixture. Bake the cake in a 375° oven for 30 to 40 minutes, or until it tests done with a toothpick. Transfer to a rack to cool. This cake is best served directly from the baking pan to prevent the topping from falling off.

YIELD: 20 servings

CHUNKY CAKE

This chocolate cake, filled with chocolate, fruit, and nuts, tastes like a Chunky candy bar. It's a big cake, which is fine since it goes fast. Give it a good start by serving it warm from the oven.

1 cup (2 sticks) butter or margarine, softened
1½ cups sugar
4 eggs
1 cup milk
2 teaspoons vanilla
2 teaspoons freeze-dried coffee, dissolved in just enough hot water to dissolve it (if using instant coffee, increase to 2½ teaspoons)

4 cups flour
¼ teaspoon salt
2 teaspoons baking soda
2 teaspoons cinnamon
⅓ cup cocoa, sifted if lumpy
6 ounces semisweet chocolate morsels
1 cup coarsely chopped walnuts
½ cup snipped dates
½ cup raisins

1. In a large bowl, cream the butter or margarine with the sugar. Beat in the eggs, then the milk, vanilla, and coffee.
2. In another bowl, stir together the flour, salt, baking soda, cinnamon, and cocoa. Beat into the creamed mixture and then stir in the chocolate, walnuts, dates, and raisins.
3. Turn the batter into a greased and floured tube pan. Bake the cake in a 350° oven for 1½ to 1¾ hours, or until it tests done with a toothpick. Transfer to a rack to cool.

YIELD: 20 to 24 servings

CHOCOLATE CHIP CAKE

A cake for kids—and for adults who still eat like kids— this golden yellow cake is flecked with ground chocolate chips and then topped with plenty more. Warm from the oven, it's a truly special treat. NOTE: While the cake is better if some of the chocolate chips are finely chopped, if you lack a blender or food processor, you may use all mini-chips in the recipe.

½ cup (1 stick) butter or margarine, softened
1½ cups sugar
2 eggs
½ teaspoon instant coffee, dissolved in 2 teaspoons hot water
1¼ cups milk
2¾ cups cake flour, or 2½ cups plus 2 tablespoons all-purpose flour

2½ teaspoons baking powder
¼ teaspoon salt
1 6-ounce package semi-sweet chocolate morsels, half of them finely chopped in blender or food processor
¼ cup coarsely chopped walnuts

1. In a large bowl, cream the butter or margarine with the sugar. Beat in the eggs, then the coffee mixture and the milk.
2. In another bowl, stir together the flour, baking powder, and salt. Beat into the creamed mixture and then stir in the finely chopped chocolate chips.
3. Turn the batter into a greased and floured 8" x 10" baking pan. Sprinkle with the remaining chocolate chips and the walnuts. Bake the cake in a 350° oven for 40 minutes, or until it tests done with a toothpick. Transfer to a rack to cool.

YIELD: 16 servings

CHOCOLATE CHIP APPLE CAKE

This recipe is such a favorite of mine (and everyone else who's ever tasted it) that I tripled the recipe and baked it for my wedding—so much more delicious than the customary tasteless white cakes commonly served at such occasions. Apples add moistness to the spicy chocolate batter, while chocolate chips further enhance the chocolate flavor. This is definitely a special cake that no chocolate fan would want to miss.

1 cup (2 sticks) butter or
   margarine, softened
2 cups sugar
3 eggs
½ cup water
1 tablespoon vanilla
2½ cups flour
2 tablespoons cocoa, sifted
   if lumpy

1 teaspoon baking soda
1 teaspoon cinnamon
1 teaspoon nutmeg
2 cups finely chopped
   peeled and cored apples
1 6-ounce package semi-
   sweet chocolate morsels

1. In a large bowl, cream the butter or margarine with the sugar. Beat in the eggs, then the water and vanilla.
2. In another bowl, stir together the flour, cocoa, baking soda, and spices. Beat into the creamed mixture and then stir in the apples and chocolate morsels.
3. Turn the batter into a greased and floured tube pan. Bake the cake in a 325° oven for 1¼ hours, or until it tests done with a toothpick. Transfer to a rack to cool.

YIELD: 16 servings

BUTTERSCOTCH CHOCOLATE CHIP CAKE

This cake tastes like those wonderful chocolate chip bar cookies translated into cake form. It's light, delicious, and very butterscotchy. For a special treat, top each serving of cake with a generous spoonful of chocolate pudding.

½ cup (1 stick) butter, softened (use real butter, if possible)
1 cup brown sugar
½ cup granulated sugar
3 eggs
1¼ cups milk
1½ teaspoons vanilla
2 cups flour

1 tablespoon baking powder
¼ teaspoon salt
½ teaspoon baking soda
½ cup finely chopped semisweet chocolate morsels
¼ cup finely chopped walnuts or pecans

1. In a bowl, cream the butter with the sugars. Beat in the eggs, then the milk and vanilla.
2. In another bowl, stir together the flour, baking powder, salt, and baking soda. Beat into the creamed mixture and then stir in the chocolate and nuts.

3. Turn the batter into a greased and floured 8" x 10" baking pan. Bake the cake in a 350° oven for 40 minutes, or until it tests done with a toothpick. Transfer to a rack to cool.

YIELD: 10 servings

HEATH BAR CAKE

For those who adore those chocolate-covered toffee Heath bars, here's a rich sour cream cake that combines the crushed bars with nutty almonds in a delightful cinnamony filling.

Cake:

½ cup (1 stick) butter or margarine, softened	1 cup white flour
¾ cup sugar	1 cup whole wheat flour
2 eggs	1½ teaspoons baking powder
1 cup sour cream	1 teaspoon baking soda
1 teaspoon vanilla	¼ teaspoon salt

Filling: (Mix all ingredients together)

¼ cup finely chopped blanched almonds	3 1¼-ounce Heath bars, crushed
1 teaspoon cinnamon	

1. In a large bowl, cream the butter or margarine with the sugar. Beat in the eggs, then the sour cream and vanilla.
2. In another bowl, stir together the flours, baking powder, baking soda, and salt. Beat into the creamed mixture.
3. Turn half the batter into a greased and floured tube pan. Sprinkle evenly with the filling and cover with the rest of the batter. Bake the cake in a 325° oven for 65 minutes, or until it tests done with a toothpick. Transfer to a rack to cool.

YIELD: 12 to 14 servings

YUGOSLAVIAN CHOCOLATE CAKE

This cake is flavored with finely ground walnuts and both unsweetened and semisweet chocolate, so it's not too sweet. This is a handy recipe to have in your collection because if you have used egg yolks for another recipe, this cake calls for egg whites only. Use a blender or food processor to grind the nuts and chocolates, being careful not to let the nuts become too oily.

½ cup (1 stick) butter or margarine, softened
¾ cup confectioners' sugar
¼ cup egg whites (about 3)
1 cup flour
¾ cup finely ground blanched almonds

2 1-ounce squares unsweetened chocolate, finely ground
2 1-ounce squares semisweet chocolate, finely ground

---

1. In a bowl, cream the butter or margarine with the confectioners' sugar. Beat in the egg whites.
2. In another bowl, stir together the flour, almonds, and chocolates. Beat into the creamed mixture.
3. Turn the batter into a greased and floured 8" x 8" pan. Bake the cake in a 350° oven for 35 to 40 minutes, or until it tests done with a toothpick. Transfer to a rack to cool.

YIELD: 16 servings

CHOCOLATE GRAHAM NUT CAKE

This recipe is adapted from an Italian torte that's served with plenty of whipped cream at festive occasions. Graham cracker crumbs and finely ground walnuts replace the usual flour in this coarse-textured, rich oblong cake. NOTE: *Grind the walnuts and chocolate separately in a blender or food processor, being careful that the nuts do not become too oily. If you lack one of these appliances, you may purchase ground walnuts and substitute mini-chocolate chips.*

6 eggs, separated
⅛ teaspoon cream of tartar
1 cup sugar, divided usage
½ teaspoon vanilla
½ cup finely crushed graham
  cracker crumbs

1 teaspoon baking powder
¼ teaspoon salt
¾ cup finely ground walnuts
¾ cup finely ground semi-
  sweet chocolate morsels

---

1. In a large bowl, beat the egg whites with the cream of tartar until stiff. Gradually beat in ¼ cup sugar until the mixture is slightly glossy. Set aside.
2. In another large bowl, beat the egg yolks (you need not clean the beaters). Gradually beat in the remaining ¾ cup sugar until the mixture is thick and pale. Beat in the vanilla.
3. In another bowl, stir together the graham cracker crumbs, baking powder, and salt. Beat into the egg yolk mixture. Stir in the walnuts and chocolate. Stir in about one-third of the egg whites to lighten the batter and then fold in the rest gently but thoroughly.
4. Turn the batter into a greased and floured 9" x 13" baking pan. Bake the cake in a 350° oven for 25 to 30 minutes, or until it tests done with a toothpick. Let cool on a rack.

YIELD: 12 servings

BITTER-CHOCOLATE ALMOND LOAF

Here's a most unusual chocolate chip cake—the chips are made from finely chopped unsweetened chocolate! You might imagine that the cake would be too bitter, but the sweet batter surrounding the chocolate provides ample sweetness. Altogether, it's a most elegant cake that has a sophisticated European flair.

5 eggs, separated
pinch salt
¾ cup sugar, divided usage
4 tablespoons (½ stick)
   butter or margarine, melted
grated rind of ½ lemon
½ teaspoon vanilla

1 cup flour
⅛ teaspoon cinnamon
3 1-ounce squares unsweetened chocolate, finely
   chopped in blender or food
   processor
1 cup ground almonds

1. In a bowl, beat the egg whites until stiff. Beat in the salt and gradually add half the sugar. The mixture should be glossy. Set aside.
2. In another bowl, beat the egg yolks with the remaining half of sugar. Beat in the melted butter, then the lemon rind and vanilla.
3. Stir together the flour and cinnamon and stir into the egg yolk mixture. Stir in half the beaten egg whites and then fold in the rest gently but thoroughly. Stir in the chocolate and almonds.
4. Turn the batter into a greased and floured 9" x 5" loaf pan. Bake the cake in a 375° oven for about 45 minutes, or until it tests done with a toothpick. Transfer to a rack to cool. Serve with whipped cream, if desired.

YIELD: 8 to 10 servings

Spice Cakes

Spices, especially the four favorites of any cake batter—cinnamon, nutmeg, ginger, and cloves—add so much warmth and fragrance to cakes of all types that you'll find them used generously throughout all the chapters of this book. But this chapter is devoted to those cakes that are so positively heady with spices, they are known and named for these flavorings. Thus, you'll encounter here gingerbreads, oatmeal spice cake, dried fruit spice cake, and other such aromatic offerings.

Spice cakes are among the most quickly put together of all cakes. The entire batter is flavored in just the few seconds it takes to measure out a teaspoon of cinnamon or a half teaspoon of nutmeg . . . and the rewards of such cakes are not only in the eating but also in the marvelous perfume they waft through the kitchen during baking.

OLD-FASHIONED GINGERBREAD

There are times when we all long for those old-fashioned, traditional desserts of our childhood. And homey gingerbread, warm from the oven and topped with whipped cream or applesauce, certainly assuages those cravings. While the cake is perhaps most fragrant and satisfying warm from the oven, it is also delicious after it has cooled to room temperature.

½ cup (1 stick) butter or margarine, softened
1 cup sugar
2 eggs
1 cup molasses
1 tablespoon lemon juice plus enough milk to equal 1 cup liquid

1 cup whole wheat flour
1 cup white flour
1 tablespoon cocoa, sifted if lumpy
2 teaspoons baking soda
2 teaspoons cinnamon
1½ teaspoons ginger
¼ teaspoon salt

1. In a large bowl, cream the butter or margarine with the sugar. Beat in the eggs, then the molasses and lemon-milk mixture.
2. In another bowl, stir together the flours, cocoa, baking soda, spices, and salt. Beat into the creamed mixture.
3. Turn the batter into a greased and floured 9" x 13" baking pan. Bake the cake in a 350° oven for 45 minutes, or until it tests done with a toothpick. Transfer to a rack to cool.

YIELD: 12 servings

CORNMEAL GINGERBREAD

This is an old New England recipe, developed when wheat flour was in short supply and cornmeal far more readily available. Yet it is still as tasty today as it was 200 years ago. The cornmeal gives the cake a pleasantly coarse texture. The procedure varies from that of most cakes, mainly because molasses replaces all of the usual sugar and because the cornmeal must be moistened by the butter and molasses mixture rather than stirred with the other dry ingredients. Like most other gingerbreads, this one is delicious warm from the oven or at room temperature.

½ cup molasses
4 tablespoons (½ stick)
   butter or margarine
1 cup cornmeal, preferably
   yellow and not
   degerminated
1 tablespoon lemon juice
   plus enough milk to equal
   1 cup liquid

½ cup whole wheat flour
1 teaspoon ginger
¼ teaspoon salt
1 teaspoon baking soda
1 egg, beaten

1. Place the molasses and butter or margarine in a large saucepan and heat until the butter melts. Remove from the heat and stir in the cornmeal, then the lemon-milk mixture.

2. In a bowl, stir together the flour, ginger, salt, and baking soda. Stir into the molasses mixture along with the egg.
3. Turn the batter into a greased and floured 8" x 8" pan. Bake in a 350° oven for 25 to 30 minutes, or until the cake tests done with a toothpick. Transfer to a rack to cool.

YIELD: 8 servings

FRESH GINGERBREAD

This is for those who like a really spicy gingerbread. Freshly grated ginger root lends an especially potent flavor to this dark cake, that's moist from the generous addition of molasses. This cake is delicious served with whipped cream.

½ cup (1 stick) butter or margarine, softened
½ cup sugar
1 egg
1 cup molasses

¼ cup freshly grated ginger root
2½ cups flour
1½ teaspoons baking soda
1 cup boiling water

1. In a bowl, cream the butter or margarine with the sugar. Beat in the egg, then the molasses and ginger root.
2. In another bowl, stir together the flour and baking soda. Beat into the ginger mixture, along with the boiling water.
3. Turn the batter into a greased and floured 8" x 8" pan. Bake the cake in a 350° oven for 50 minutes, or until it tests done with a toothpick. Let cool on a rack.

YIELD: 9 servings

VERMONT GINGERBREAD

Maple syrup replaces the customary molasses in this old New England recipe. The result is a lighter, milder cake that's ideal for those who find the strong flavor of molasses over-powering. The more economical maple-flavored syrup may be used in place of the real syrup. Like most gingerbreads, this is delicious warm from the oven.

3 eggs
½ cup brown sugar
9 tablespoons (1 stick plus
    1 tablespoon) butter or
    margarine, melted
1 cup maple syrup
1¼ cups white flour
1¼ cups whole wheat flour
1 tablespoon ginger

2 teaspoons cinnamon
½ teaspoon ground cloves
½ teaspoon nutmeg
1 teaspoon baking soda
1 teaspoon baking powder
¼ teaspoon salt
1 tablespoon minced can-
    died orange peel

---

1. In a bowl, beat the eggs. Gradually beat in the brown sugar. Beat in the melted butter or margarine, then the maple syrup.
2. In another bowl, stir together the flours, spices, baking soda, baking powder, and salt. Beat into the maple mixture, then stir in the orange peel.
3. Turn the batter into a greased and floured 8" x 10" baking pan. Bake the cake in a 350° oven for 35 to 40 minutes, or until it tests done with a toothpick. Let cool on a rack.

YIELD: 12 servings

SCOTTISH GINGERBREAD

Most of the cakes Americans commonly eat were developed by American cooks and, even now, are quite rarely found beyond the borders of this country. Gingerbread, however, is one exception; even very early British cookbooks give recipes for this special type of spice cake. This version is from Scotland and is unique because of the addition of beer and candied orange peel.

1 cup (2 sticks) butter or margarine, softened
½ cup sugar
¾ cup molasses
2 eggs
1 cup beer, measured without foam
1¾ cups white flour
1¾ cups whole wheat flour
1 tablespoon ginger

1 teaspoon cinnamon
¼ teaspoon ground cloves
¼ teaspoon nutmeg
1 teaspoon baking soda
½ cup raisins
½ cup diced candied orange peel
½ cup finely chopped almonds

1. In a large bowl, cream the butter or margarine with the sugar and molasses. Beat in the eggs, then the beer.
2. In another bowl, stir together the flours, spices, and baking soda. Beat into the creamed mixture, then stir in the raisins, orange peel, and almonds.
3. Turn the batter into a greased and floured 9" x 13" baking pan. Bake the cake in a 325° oven for 40 minutes, or until it tests done with a toothpick. Transfer to a rack to cool.

YIELD: 20 servings

GERMAN CHRISTMAS GINGERBREAD

Far more elaborate than our own frugal American ginger-breads, this festive cake is meant to be served throughout the Christmas holidays. The honey makes it a particularly moist and long-keeping cake. Sour cream, orange liqueur, and plenty of spices add to its fine texture and flavor.

1 cup (2 sticks) butter or margarine, softened
2 cups brown sugar
3 eggs
⅔ cup honey
¼ cup orange liqueur, such as Cointreau
1 cup sour cream
½ cup orange juice
1⅔ cup white flour

1 cup whole wheat flour
4 teaspoons baking powder
2 teaspoons ginger
1 teaspoon cinnamon
¼ teaspoon nutmeg
¼ teaspoon ground cloves
1 cup raisins
1 cup slivered blanched almonds

---

1. In a large bowl, cream the butter or margarine with the brown sugar. Beat in the eggs, then the honey, orange liqueur, sour cream, and orange juice.
2. In another bowl, stir together the flours, baking powder, and spices. Beat into the creamed mixture and then stir in the raisins and almonds.
3. Turn the batter into a greased and floured tube pan. Bake the cake in a 350° oven for 1 hour and 20 minutes, or until it tests done with a toothpick. Transfer to a rack to cool.

YIELD: 16 servings

GERMAN SPICE CAKE WITH BEER

This is a wonderfully fragrant cake—full of spices and the heady taste of beer. It's put together with remarkable speed because it contains no eggs and the butter is melted in the beer and molasses.

1½ cups (1 12-ounce can) beer
1 cup molasses
½ cup (1 stick) butter or margarine
1½ cups raisins
1½ cups whole wheat flour
1⅓ cups white flour

¼ teaspoon salt
1 tablespoon baking powder
¼ teaspoon baking soda
1 teaspoon cinnamon
¼ teaspoon nutmeg
¼ teaspoon ground cloves
½ cup coarsely chopped walnuts

1. In a large saucepan, heat the beer, molasses, and butter or margarine until the butter melts. Remove from the heat and stir in the raisins.
2. In a bowl, stir together the flours, salt, baking powder, baking soda, and spices. Stir into the liquid mixture and then stir in the walnuts.
3. Turn the batter into a greased and floured tube pan. Bake the cake in a 350° oven for 50 minutes, or until it tests done with a toothpick. Let cool on a rack.

YIELD: 12 to 14 servings

TORTA PARADISO (ITALIAN SPICE CAKE)

Red wine gives this spice cake a lovely color and even more aroma than usual.

½ cup (1 stick) butter or margarine, softened
1¼ cups sugar
2 eggs
¾ cup dry red wine
1 tablespoon molasses
¼ cup milk
1½ teaspoons vanilla
2 cups flour
2½ tablespoons cornstarch

1 tablespoon baking powder
1 teaspoon cinnamon
½ teaspoon nutmeg
¼ teaspoon ground cloves
¼ teaspoon ginger
¼ teaspoon salt
½ cup finely chopped almonds

1. In a large bowl, cream the butter or margarine with the sugar. Beat in the eggs, then the wine, molasses, milk, and vanilla.
2. In another bowl, stir together the flour, cornstarch, baking powder, spices, and salt. Beat into the creamed mixture and then stir in the nuts.
3. Turn the batter into a greased and floured 8" x 10" baking pan. Bake the cake in a 350° oven for 35 to 40 minutes, or until it tests done with a toothpick. Transfer to a rack to cool.

YIELD: 12 to 14 servings

SPICED HONEY CHIFFON CAKE

Coffee flavors this well-textured honey spice cake. A gala tube cake, it's a dessert for impressing guests. A scoop of coffee ice cream on each serving makes it even more festive.

4 eggs, separated
¼ teaspoon cream of tartar
1 cup sugar, divided usage
¼ cup salad oil
1⅓ cups honey, dissolved in
  1⅓ cups hot strong coffee
3½ cups flour

2½ teaspoons baking powder
1 teaspoon baking soda
1 teaspoon cinnamon
⅛ teaspoon ground cloves
⅛ teaspoon ginger
⅛ teaspoon salt

---

1. In a bowl, beat the egg whites with the cream of tartar until stiff. Gradually beat in ½ cup sugar until the mixture is glossy. Set aside.
2. In a large bowl, beat the egg yolks. Gradually beat in the remaining ½ cup sugar. Then beat in the oil and honey-coffee mixture.
3. In another bowl, stir together the flour, baking powder, baking soda, spices, and salt. Beat into the honey mixture. Stir in about one-third of the egg whites and then fold in the rest gently but thoroughly.
4. Turn the batter into a greased and floured tube pan. Bake the cake in a 350° oven for 1¼ hours, or until it tests done with a toothpick. Transfer to a rack to cool.

YIELD: 16 to 20 servings

MOCHA SPICE CAKE

Coffee and cocoa lend a dark color and extra flavor to this quickly-put-together spice cake.

1½ cups strong coffee
1½ cups sugar, divided usage
1½ tablespoons cocoa, sifted
   if lumpy
6 tablespoons (¾ stick)
   butter or margarine,
   softened
2 eggs

½ teaspoon vanilla
1½ cups flour
½ teaspoon baking soda
1½ teaspoons baking powder
¼ teaspoon salt
¾ teaspoon cinnamon
¾ teaspoon nutmeg
¼ teaspoon ground cloves

1. Place the coffee, ¾ cup sugar, and cocoa in a saucepan. Simmer 10 minutes, stirring until the sugar dissolves. Remove from the heat.
2. In a bowl, cream the butter or margarine with the remaining ¾ cup sugar. Beat in the eggs, then the vanilla and the coffee mixture.
3. In another bowl, stir together the flour, baking soda, baking powder, salt, and spices. Beat into the coffee batter.
4. Turn the batter into a greased and floured 8" x 8" baking pan. Bake the cake in a 350° oven for 50 minutes, or until it tests done with a toothpick. Let cool on a rack.

YIELD: 9 servings

OLD-FASHIONED TOMATO SOUP SPICE CAKE

Although the name of this cake definitely sounds weird, don't be put off by it. The tomato soup lends a pleasingly tart flavor to the cake, but not a real tomato taste. It also adds a hearty body and attractive color. This is a traditional recipe, many, many generations old.

½ cup (1 stick) butter or margarine, softened
1⅓ cups sugar
2 eggs
1 can (10¾ ounces) condensed tomato soup
¼ cup water
2 cups flour

4 teaspoons baking powder
1 teaspoons baking soda
1½ teaspoons nutmeg
1 teaspoon cinnamon
½ teaspoon ground cloves
⅔ cup raisins
⅔ cup coarsely chopped walnuts

1. In a large bowl, cream the butter or margarine with the sugar. Beat in the eggs, then the tomato soup and water.
2. In another bowl, stir together the flour, baking powder, baking soda, and spices. Beat into the tomato mixture and then stir in the raisins and walnuts.
3. Turn the batter into a greased and floured 9" x 13" baking pan. Bake the cake in a 350° oven for 40 minutes, or until it tests done with a toothpick. Transfer to a rack to cool.

YIELD: 20 servings

ENGLISH CRUMB CAKE

This rich spice cake, flavored with apple cider and topped with a crunchy topping, is delicious served right from the oven.

Cake Batter:
2 eggs
½ cup brown sugar
¼ cup molasses
1¼ cups apple cider (or
   substitute apple juice)
1¼ cups white flour

1 cup whole wheat flour
2 teaspoons baking powder
¼ teaspoon baking soda
¼ teaspoon salt
½ teaspoon cinnamon

Topping:
3 tablespoons apple butter
3 tablespoons butter or
   margarine, softened
6 tablespoons flour
3 tablespoons granulated
   sugar

3 tablespoons finely chopped
   walnuts
½ teaspoon cinnamon

-----

1. In a large bowl, beat the eggs. Beat in the brown sugar until the mixture is thick. Beat in the molasses and apple cider.
2. In another bowl, stir together the flours, baking powder, baking soda, salt, and cinnamon. Beat into the apple mixture.
3. Turn the batter into a greased and floured 8" x 10" baking pan. Bake in a 325° oven for 25 minutes.
4. While the cake is baking, combine all topping ingredients except the apple butter. After 25 minutes, remove the cake from the oven, spread with the apple butter, and sprinkle with the topping. Bake 20 minutes longer, or until it tests done with a toothpick. Transfer to a rack to cool. Because the topping is quite crumbly, it is best to serve the cake

directly from the baking pan; if you tip it upside down, the topping may fall off.

YIELD: 12 servings

JAM CAKE

I have baked this moist, tender spice cake with nearly every type of jam imaginable—raspberry, pineapple, fig, strawberry, etc.—and every time it has been a delightfully flavored cake. You can also use marmalade, but not jelly, which has a different consistency than jams. The red jams also lend a beautiful pink tint to the cake.

6 tablespoons (¾ stick) butter
  or margarine, softened
1 cup brown sugar
2 eggs
3 tablespoons sour cream
1 cup jam of any flavor

1½ cups flour
1 teaspoon baking powder
½ teaspoon baking soda
½ teaspoon ground cloves
1 teaspoon cinnamon
1 teaspoon nutmeg

1. In a bowl, cream the butter or margarine with the brown sugar. Beat in the eggs, then the sour cream and jam.
2. In another bowl, stir together the flour, baking powder, baking soda, and spices. Beat into the jam mixture.
3. Turn the batter into a greased and floured 9" x 5" loaf pan. Bake the cake in a 350° oven for about 50 minutes, or until it tests done with a toothpick. Transfer to a rack to cool.

YIELD: 8 to 10 slices

MINCEMEAT SPICE CAKE

A blender or food processor makes this cake a snap to whip up, which is nice since it makes a marvelous gift during the holidays. Condensed mincemeat is very hard but can be chopped finely with a knife if you lack one of these appliances. If you do chop the mincemeat by hand, cream the butter or margarine with the brown sugar and then beat in the egg, milk, and vanilla. Stir in the mincemeat and then proceed with step 2 of the recipe.

1 cup (2 sticks) butter or
   margarine, softened
1 cup brown sugar
1 egg
½ cup milk
1 teaspoon vanilla
1 9-ounce box condensed
   mincemeat

2 cups flour
¼ teaspoon salt
½ teaspoon cinnamon
¼ teaspoon nutmeg
1 teaspoon baking powder
1 teaspoon baking soda

1. Place the butter or margarine, brown sugar, egg, milk, and vanilla in a blender or food processor. Process until quite smooth. Add the mincemeat, coarsely broken up, and process until fully mixed in.
2. In a large bowl, stir together the flour, salt, spices, baking powder, and baking soda. Add the liquid ingredients and stir until well combined.
3. Turn the batter into a greased and floured 9" x 13" baking pan. Bake the cake in a 350° oven for 30 minutes, or until it tests done with a toothpick. Transfer to a rack to cool.

YIELD: 20 servings

GLAZED PRUNE SPICE CAKE

Here's an old-fashioned cake with a delightful glaze that seeps into the baked cake to make it rich and moist.

NOTE: *To cut down on the preparation time, measure all ingredients that go into both the batter and the glaze at the same time. Thus, when you add the sugar to the batter bowl, add sugar also to the saucepan. Do the same for the baking soda, butter or margarine, lemon-milk mixture, and vanilla. This will save having to measure these ingredients twice.*

Cake Batter:

3 eggs
1½ cups sugar
½ cup (1 stick) butter or
    margarine, melted
1 tablespoon lemon juice
    plus enough milk to equal
    1 cup liquid
1 teaspoon vanilla

2 cups flour
1 teaspoon baking soda
1 teaspoon cinnamon
1 teaspoon nutmeg
¼ teaspoon salt
1 cup chopped dried
    prunes

Glaze:

1 cup sugar
½ teaspoon baking soda
½ cup (1 stick) butter or
    margarine
1½ teaspoons lemon juice
    plus enough milk to equal
    ½ cup liquid

1 tablespoon honey
½ teaspoon vanilla

---

1. In a large bowl, beat the eggs. Beat in the sugar until the mixture is thick and pale. Beat in the melted butter or margarine, then the lemon-milk mixture and vanilla.
2. In another bowl, stir together the flour, baking soda, spices, and salt. Beat into the liquid mixture and then stir in the prunes.
3. Turn the batter into a greased and floured 9" x 13" baking

pan. Bake the cake in a 300° oven for 50 minutes, or until it tests done with a toothpick.

4. While the cake is baking, mix all glaze ingredients in a saucepan. Bring to a boil, stirring. Cook until thick and frothy, about 2 minutes. As soon as the cake comes from the oven, pour the glaze over it. NOTE: This cake keeps well for days if stored in the refrigerator. It is even better a day after baking, since the glaze has had plenty of time to permeate the cake.

YIELD: 20 servings

HOLIDAY FRUIT AND NUT SPICE CAKE

This luscious spice cake is so filled with nuts and dried and candied fruits that it is a perfect offering for holiday entertaining and is especially ideal for those who want a festive cake but aren't fond of traditional fruit cakes.

¾ cup (1½ sticks) butter or margarine, softened
1⅓ cups sugar
3 eggs
¼ cup milk
2 tablespoons dark rum
2 tablespoons molasses
2 cups flour
1 teaspoon baking powder
¼ teaspoon salt

¼ teaspoon nutmeg
½ teaspoon cinnamon
⅛ teaspoon ground cloves
1 cup coarsely chopped walnuts
1 cup diced candied orange peel
½ cup golden raisins
½ cup diced dried prunes

1. In a large bowl, cream the butter or margarine with the sugar. Beat in the eggs, then the milk, rum, and molasses.
2. In another bowl, stir together the flour, baking powder, salt, and spices. Beat into the creamed mixture and then stir in the nuts, orange peel, and dried fruits.

3. Turn the batter into a greased and floured 8" x 10" baking pan. Bake in a 300° oven for 65 minutes, or until the cake tests done with a toothpick. Let cool on a rack.
YIELD: 16 servings

GERMAN ANISE CAKE

Anise, of course, lends a licorice-like flavor to this butter-less, sponge-type cake. Since there is no leavening in the cake, it is the stiffly beaten egg whites that give it a light texture. This egg-rich cake makes a fine Christmas offering to friends.

4 eggs, separated
1 cup sugar
1 tablespoon anise seed

1 tablespoon lemon juice
¼ teaspoon salt
1 cup flour

1. In a bowl, beat the egg whites until stiff, and set aside.
2. In another bowl, beat the egg yolks. Gradually beat in the sugar. When done, the mixture should be thick and pale. Beat in the anise, lemon juice, salt, and flour. Stir in about one-third of the egg whites to lighten the batter and then fold in the rest gently but thoroughly.
3. Spread the batter evenly in a greased and floured 8" x 10" baking pan. Bake in a 375° oven for about 25 minutes, or until the cake tests done with a toothpick. Let cool on a rack. This cake is most commonly served cut into strips about 1" x 2".
YIELD: 40 strips

GINGERED VODKA CAKE

Although you'll find no powdered spices in this cake, the crystallized ginger exudes such a powerful flavor that this recipe certainly belongs within this chapter. Of all the cakes in the book, this most special and attractive tube cake is perhaps my favorite; and I bake it whenever I have leftover egg whites from another dish. While most cakes that call for many egg whites and no yolks are angel food cakes, because this recipe also calls for butter (and real butter is a must here), the result is a very delicate pound-type cake. The ground pecans add a wonderful flavor of their own; and the taste of vodka permeates all.

NOTE: Leftover egg whites keep well for months in the freezer. I generally keep a plastic container of them in the freezer and keep track of the number of egg whites I add to it. When I have enough, I defrost them all and bake this cake.

1 cup (2 sticks) butter,
  softened (use real butter,
  if possible)
1¾ cups sugar
¾ cup egg whites (about 7)
¾ cup vodka
2 teaspoons vanilla

2¾ cups flour
1 tablespoon baking powder
¾ cup finely chopped or
  ground pecans
½ cup finely diced
  crystallized ginger

---

1. In a large bowl, cream the butter with the sugar. Beat in the egg whites, then the vodka and vanilla.
2. In another bowl, stir together the flour and baking powder. Beat into the vodka mixture. Stir in the pecans and ginger.
3. Turn the batter into a greased and floured tube pan. Bake the cake in a 300° oven for 1½ hours, or until it tests done with a toothpick. Let the cake cool on a rack.

YIELD: 16 to 18 servings

BRITISH CARAWAY CAKE

We so often encounter caraway seeds in savory foods that they may seem out of place in a sweet cake. Yet this delightful, caraway-flavored sponge cake is quite at home on any British tea trolley. The lemon rind adds a nice accent to the caraway.

5 eggs	2 teaspoons caraway seeds
1 cup granulated sugar	1 cup plus 3 tablespoons
2 teaspoons water	flour
2 tablespoons grated lemon	½ cup confectioners' sugar
rind	

1. In a bowl, beat the eggs. Gradually beat in the granulated sugar. When done, the mixture should be thick and pale. Beat in the water, lemon rind, and caraway seeds. Gently beat in the flour.
2. Turn the batter into a greased and floured tube pan. Sprinkle with the confectioners' sugar. Bake the cake in a 350° oven for 50 minutes, or until it tests done with a toothpick. Let cool on a rack.

YIELD: 14 servings

POPPY SEED CAKE

The subtle, nutty flavor of poppy seeds is delectable in this rich, honey-sweetened, sour cream tube cake.

½ cup poppy seeds
⅓ cup honey
¼ cup water
4 eggs, separated
1 cup (2 sticks) butter or
  margarine, softened (use
  at least half real butter, if
  possible)

1½ cups sugar
2 teaspoons vanilla
1 cup sour cream
2½ cups flour
1 teaspoon baking soda
¼ teaspoon salt

1. Place the poppy seeds, honey, and water in a saucepan. Cook, stirring occasionally, 5 minutes. Remove from heat and set aside.
2. Beat the egg whites until stiff, and set aside.
3. In a large bowl, cream the butter with the sugar. Beat in the egg yolks, then the vanilla, sour cream, and poppy seed mixture.
4. In another bowl, stir together the flour, baking soda, and salt. Beat into the poppy seed mixture. Stir in about one-third of the egg whites to lighten the batter and fold in the rest gently but thoroughly.
5. Turn the batter into a greased and floured tube pan. Bake the cake in a 350° oven for about 1 hour, or until it tests done with a toothpick. Let cool on a rack.

YIELD: 12 to 14 servings

TOASTED SESAME CAKE

The beaten egg whites give this delicate tube cake a fine texture, while the toasted sesame seeds add an exotic flavor. Since sesame seeds can be expensive when needed in this quantity, try to purchase them in bulk (from a mail-order spice house, a health food store, or an ethnic grocery store, such as one specializing in Greek foods).

1¼ cups sesame seeds
½ cup milk
4 eggs, separated
1 cup (2 sticks) butter, softened (use real butter, if possible)

1¼ cups sugar
1 teaspoon vanilla
1½ cups flour
2 teaspoons baking powder

1. Toast the sesame seeds in a dry skillet until they turn a very pale brown. Remove skillet from heat. Gradually add the milk.
2. In a bowl, beat the egg whites until stiff, and set aside.
3. In a large bowl, cream the butter with the sugar. Beat in the egg yolks, then the vanilla and sesame seed mixture.
4. In a small bowl, stir the flour with the baking powder. Beat into the creamed mixture. Stir in about one-third of the beaten egg whites and then fold in the rest gently but thoroughly.
5. Turn the batter into a greased and floured tube pan. Bake the cake in a 350° oven for about 65 minutes, or until it tests done with a toothpick. Let cool on a rack.

YIELD: 10 to 12 servings

CARDAMON SHERRY CAKE

Although cardamon is not a common ingredient in this country, it is a popular spice in Scandanavian pastries, as well as an almost essential addition to Indian curries. The taste is a bit like nutmeg, but somewhat more piquant. Along with this fragrant spice, sherry flavors the batter of this attractive tube cake, and additional sherry is sprinkled over the finished cake. If you are serving guests, try topping each slice with whipped cream that has been lightly spiced with cardamon (use ⅛ teaspoon cardamon to 1 cup heavy cream, whipped, or to taste).

NOTE: *Be certain to use dry cocktail sherry, not cooking sherry, which contains too much salt.*

6 tablespoons (¾ stick) butter or margarine, softened	¼ cup milk
	1 teaspoon lemon juice
1⅓ cups sugar, divided usage	1½ cups flour
2 eggs	1 teaspoon cardamon
⅓ cup plus 3 tablespoons dry sherry, divided usage	1½ teaspoons baking powder
	¼ teaspoon salt

1. In a bowl, cream the butter or margarine with 1 cup of the sugar. Beat in the eggs, then ⅓ cup sherry, the milk, and the lemon juice.
2. In another bowl, stir together the flour, cardamon, baking powder, and salt. Beat into the creamed mixture.
3. Turn the batter into a greased and floured tube pan. Bake the cake in a 300° oven for 40 minutes, or until it tests done with a toothpick.
4. Meanwhile, heat the remaining 3 tablespoons sherry with the remaining ⅓ cup sugar in a small saucepan just until the sugar dissolves. Pour over the cake as soon as it comes from the oven. Transfer to a rack to cool.

YIELD: 10 servings

Bar Cakes

Although most cookbooks classify bars as cookies, to my mind they are really extra-thin cakes. The batter is made in the same way as for cake batters; and they require none of that tedious shaping or dropping and careful surveillance over the baking that are the hallmark of true cookies.

There is also a rather fine line between a thin oblong cake and a bar cake. So for these rasons, along with the fact that these are among the chewiest and most flavorful of cakes, I have decided to devote a chapter of this book to my favorite examples of cakes of this type.

Bar cakes offer two additional advantages. Because they are thin, they usually bake in less time than other cakes (and therefore are ready to be consumed even sooner). Most bar cakes are also quite sturdy and so pack and mail well for gift-giving. As an added bonus, because they are cut into small squares, it's easy to make one pan and give half as a gift, while still saving some for your own enjoyment.

BROWNIES, WITH VARIATIONS

The secret to great, chewy brownies is beating the eggs with the sugar until the mixture turns very thick and pale. Very slightly underbaking the brownies, too, makes for especially luscious, dark squares. I, personally, do not care for nuts in brownies; I want nothing to interfere between me and the meltingly rich chocolate taste. But others, I know, feel quite differently and therefore nuts are an optional ingredient.

Below is a classic brownie recipe, for irresistible "can't-stop-with-just-one" brownies. Also included are variations: fabulous Cheesecake Brownies (even richer than the traditional version); Cherry Brownies (like Black Forest Cherry Cake with only ten percent of the work); and Spicy Mocha Brownies (for those who like the added aroma of coffee).

2 1-ounce squares
  unsweetened chocolate
⅓ cup (5⅓ tablespoons) butter
  or margarine
2 eggs
1 cup sugar

1 teaspoon vanilla
⅔ cup flour
½ teaspoon baking powder
¼ teaspoon salt
½ cup chopped walnuts or
  pecans, optional

1. In a small saucepan, over very low heat, melt the chocolate and butter or margarine.
2. In a bowl, beat the eggs. Gradually beat in the sugar. When done, the mixture should be thick and pale. Beat in the melted chocolate mixture and the vanilla.
3. In another bowl, stir together the flour, baking powder, and salt. Beat into the chocolate mixture and stir in the nuts if desired.
4. Turn the batter into a greased and floured 8" x 8" baking pan. Bake the brownies in a 350° oven for 25 minutes. A toothpick inserted in the center should come out almost, but not completely, dry. Let cool on a rack and then cut into squares.

YIELD: 9 brownies, about 1½ inches square

Cheesecake Brownies: Make basic brownie batter. In another bowl, beat together 1 8-ounce package cream cheese, softened; ⅓ cup sugar; 1 egg; and ½ teaspoon vanilla. Pour half the brownie batter into the pan, cover with the cream cheese mixture, and then cover with the remaining brownie batter. These will require about 5 minutes more baking time because they are thicker.

Cherry Brownies: Make basic brownie batter. Fold in 1 1-pound can well-drained sour or dark sweet pitted cherries as the last step. These will also require about 5 minutes additional baking time because of the moisture of the cherries.

Spicy Mocha Brownies: Add to the dry ingredients 2 teaspoons instant coffee powder. Freeze-dried crystals should not be substituted as they don't combine as well with the dry ingredients.

MILK CHOCOLATE OATMEAL BARS

These chewy bars are flavored with milk chocolate. You may use either milk chocolate morsels or ordinary milk chocolate candy bars. Coffee imparts a pleasing mocha accent.

½ cup (1 stick) butter or margarine, softened
1 cup brown sugar
2 eggs
6 ounces milk chocolate, melted
½ cup evaporated milk

1½ cups flour
2 teaspoons baking powder
¼ teaspoon salt
2 teaspoons instant coffee powder
1 cup rolled oats

1. In a bowl, cream the butter or margarine with the brown sugar. Beat in the eggs, then the melted chocolate and evaporated milk.
2. In another bowl, stir together the flour, baking powder, salt, coffee, and oats. Beat into the chocolate mixture.
3. Spread the batter evenly in a greased and floured 9" x 13" pan. Bake the bars in a 375° oven for 25 minutes, or until a toothpick inserted in the center comes out clean. Let cool on a rack and then cut into bars.

YIELD: 24 2-inch bars

CHOCOLATE CREAM CHEESE BARS

These are for people who like cakelike brownies. Rather than being soft, moist, and chewy, these bars are dense and thick, with a rich cream cheese flavor.

10 tablespoons (1 stick plus
   2 tablespoons) butter or
   margarine, softened
4 ounces cream cheese,
   softened
1 cup brown sugar
3 eggs
1 teaspoon vanilla

1½ cups flour
1 teaspoon baking powder
¼ teaspoon salt
6 tablespoons cocoa, sifted
   if lumpy
¾ cup coarsely chopped
   walnuts

1. In a bowl, cream the butter or margarine and cream cheese with the brown sugar. Beat in the eggs, then the vanilla.
2. In another bowl, stir together the flour, baking powder, salt, and cocoa. Beat these dry ingredients into the creamed mixture. Stir in the walnuts.
3. Turn the batter into a greased and floured 8" x 10" baking pan. Bake in a 350° oven for 25 to 30 minutes, or until a toothpick inserted in the center comes out clean. Transfer to a rack to cool and then cut into squares.

YIELD: 20 2-inch squares

EXTRA-MOIST CHOCOLATE BANANA BARS

These dark bars are so moist, they almost stick to the serving plate. But any messiness in eating is well worth it because this treat is such a delectable combination of sweet, fruity bananas and lovely chocolate.

½ cup (1 stick) butter or
   margarine, softened
¼ cup granulated sugar
½ cup brown sugar
1 egg
¼ cup milk
1 cup mashed ripe bananas
1 6-ounce package semisweet
   chocolate morsels, melted

1 cup flour
1 cup bran cereal, such as
   All-Bran
½ teaspoon baking powder
¼ teaspoon baking soda
¼ teaspoon salt
½ teaspoon cinnamon

1. In a bowl, cream the butter or margarine with the sugars. Beat in the egg, then the milk, bananas, and melted chocolate.
2. In another bowl, stir together the flour, bran, baking powder, baking soda, salt, and cinnamon. Beat into the banana mixture.
3. Turn the batter into a greased and floured 9" x 13" baking pan. Bake the bars in a 350° oven for 25 minutes, or until they test done with a toothpick. (Because these bars are so moist, the toothpick will be almost, but not quite, clean.) Let cool on a rack and then cut into bars.

YIELD: 24 2-inch bars

CRANBERRY CHOCOLATE BARS

These spicy bars taste like fruity brownies. The canned cranberry sauce is most convenient and makes this recipe a breeze to whip up.

¾ cup (1½ sticks) butter or margarine, softened
¾ cup granulated sugar
¾ cup brown sugar
2 eggs
1 teaspoon vanilla
4 ounces (about ⅔ cup) semisweet chocolate morsels, melted
1 cup whole-berry cranberry sauce

1½ teaspoons lemon juice plus enough milk to equal ½ cup liquid
1 cup whole wheat flour
1 cup minus 2 tablespoons white flour
½ teaspoon baking soda
¾ teaspoon ginger
¾ teaspoon cinnamon
½ teaspoon ground cloves

1. In a large bowl, cream the butter or margarine with the sugars. Beat in the eggs, then the vanilla, melted chocolate, cranberry sauce, and lemon-milk mixture.
2. In another bowl, stir together the flours, baking soda, and spices. Beat into the creamed mixture.
3. Spread the batter evenly in a greased and floured 9" x 13" baking pan. Bake the bars in a 350° oven for about 40 minutes, or until a toothpick inserted in the center comes out clean. Transfer to a rack to cool; and when cool, cut into bars.

YIELD: 24 2-inch bars

WALNUT FUDGE BARS

Be forewarned: These bars are addicting! The top and bottom crusts are like chewy oatmeal cookies; and in between there's a candy-like fudge layer.

Cake Layers:

6 tablespoons (¾ stick)
    butter or margarine,
    softened
1 cup brown sugar
1 egg

1 teaspoon vanilla
1 cup flour
⅛ teaspoon salt
1¼ teaspoons baking powder
1½ cups rolled oats

Fudge Layer:

1 6-ounce package semisweet
    chocolate morsels
½ cup sweetened condensed
    milk (not evaporated)
1 tablespoon butter or
    margarine

1 teaspoon vanilla
¾ cup coarsely chopped
    walnuts

1. In a medium bowl, cream the butter or margarine with the brown sugar. Beat in the egg and vanilla.
2. In another bowl, stir together the flour, salt, baking powder, and oats. Beat into the creamed mixture.
3. Press two-thirds of the batter into a greased 8" x 10" pan. (The easiest way to do this is to lightly flour your fingertips and use your hands to press evenly.)
4. Melt the chocolate with the milk and butter in a small saucepan. Remove from the heat and stir in the vanilla. Spread evenly over the bottom crust. Drop the remaining batter by small spoonfuls over the fudge layer and then sprinkle the walnuts over all.
5. Bake the bars in a 350° oven for 35 minutes, or until a toothpick inserted in the center comes out clean. Transfer to a rack to cool and then cut into bars.

YIELD: 20 1-inch squares

POLISH CHOCOLATE ALMOND BARS

The true name of this cake is "Mazurek," and there are dozens of versions of these extremely rich chocolate- and nut-filled bars. Because they are so exceedingly buttery, you'll find that a single recipe goes a long way. For family pleasure or added to the fanciest dessert buffet, these bars will be appreciated by anyone with a sweet tooth.

The preparation varies slightly in this recipe because the bars are baked in two stages. While the bottom layer is baking, prepare the top layer. Altogether, your work in the kitchen will still remain within 30 minutes.

Bottom Layer:

1⅛ cups (2¼ sticks) butter, softened (use real butter, if possible)
1½ cups sugar
3 whole eggs plus 4 egg yolks

1½ cups flour
½ teaspoon salt
1 cup sliced blanched almonds

Top Layer:

4 egg whites
¾ cup sugar
1 teaspoon cocoa, sifted if lumpy
1 cup raisins

1 cup sliced blanched almonds
1 cup chopped walnuts
½ cup semisweet chocolate morsels

1. In a bowl, cream the butter with the sugar. Beat in the eggs and egg yolks, then the flour and salt. Stir in the almonds. Spread the batter evenly in an 11" x 16" jelly roll pan. Bake this layer in a 300° oven for 35 minutes. Let cool 10 minutes.

2. Meanwhile, beat the egg whites until stiff (use a clean beater). Gradually beat in the sugar. When done, the mixture should be glossy. Beat in the cocoa, then stir in the raisins, almonds, walnuts, and chocolate. Spread the mix-

ture evenly over the baked layer. Continue baking in a 300°
oven 15 minutes longer.
3. Transfer the pan to a rack to cool. Then cut into bars.
YIELD: 48 2-inch squares

MOCHA-CRUNCH YOGURT BARS

*A rich, chewy oatmeal crust forms the bottom layer of these
lusciously moist, brownie-like mocha bars. The yogurt in the
batter adds to their richness, and the effect is almost like eating a wonderful form of fudge.*

Bottom Layer: (Mix all ingredients together well)

6 tablespoons (¾ stick) butter or margarine, melted	½ cup flour
	½ cup brown sugar
1 cup rolled oats	½ teaspoon cinnamon

Cake Layer:

10 tablespoons (1 stick plus 2 tablespoons) butter or margarine, softened	1½ teaspoons freeze-dried coffee crystals (or 2 teaspoons powdered instant coffee)
1 cup granulated sugar	
2 eggs	½ teaspoon baking soda
1 cup yogurt	¼ teaspoon baking powder
1 teaspoon vanilla	¼ teaspoon salt
1 cup flour	¼ cup finely chopped walnuts
6 tablespoons cocoa, sifted if lumpy	

1. Spread the mixture for the bottom layer evenly in a greased
    and floured 8" x 10" baking pan. Bake in a 350° oven for
    10 minutes.
2. Meanwhile, cream the butter or margarine with the sugar.
    Beat in the eggs, then the yogurt and vanilla.

3. In another bowl, stir together the flour, cocoa, coffee, baking soda, baking powder, and salt. Beat into the creamed mixture, and then stir in the nuts.
4. Spread the batter over the baked bottom layer and bake 35 to 40 minutes longer, or until a toothpick inserted in the center comes out clean. Transfer to a rack to cool and then cut into bars.

YIELD: 16 2-inch by 2½-inch bars

PUDDING BARS

Not your usual pudding-plus-cake-mix cake, these bars rely on chocolate pudding mix for flavor. Dates and coconut make them extra appealing.

2 eggs
½ cup sugar
6 tablespoons (¾ stick) butter
    or margarine, melted
1 teaspoon vanilla
½ cup flour

2 packages (about 3¾ ounces
    each) regular chocolate
    fudge or chocolate pudding
    and pie filling mix
½ cup chopped dates
½ cup shredded coconut

1. In a bowl, beat the eggs. Gradually beat in the sugar, then the melted butter or margarine and vanilla.
2. In another bowl, stir together the flour and pudding mix. Beat into the liquid ingredients and then stir in the dates and coconut.
3. Turn the batter into a greased and floured 8" x 10" baking pan. Bake the bars in a 325° oven for 25 to 30 minutes, or until a toothpick inserted in the center comes out clean. Let cool on a rack and then cut into bars.

YIELD: 12 1½-inch by 4-inch bars

BANANA MOLASSES BARS

Molasses makes these moist, fruity bars even more delectable. Oats, wheat germ, and whole wheat flour make for a nutritious snack treat that's especially good when you serve these bars warm from the oven.

1 cup (2 sticks) butter or margarine, softened	2 large, ripe bananas, mashed
¾ cup brown sugar	2 cups whole wheat flour
2 eggs	¾ cup rolled oats
¼ cup molasses	2 teaspoons baking powder
¼ cup honey	¼ teaspoon salt
	½ cup wheat germ

1. In a bowl, cream the butter or margarine with the brown sugar. Beat in the eggs, then the molasses, honey, and mashed banana.
2. In another bowl, stir together the flour, oats, baking powder, salt, and wheat germ. Beat into the banana mixture.
3. Spread the batter evenly in a greased and floured 9" x 13" baking pan. Bake the bars in a 375° oven for 35 to 40 minutes, or until they test done with a toothpick (because these bars are so moist, the toothpick will be almost, but not quite, clean). Let cool on a rack and then cut into bars.

YIELD: 24 2-inch bars

PEANUT BANANA BARS

Peanut butter and banana sandwiches are among the most pleasant memories of my childhood. Here, these two well-matched flavors pair up in a rich, crunchy bar.

4 tablespoons (½ stick)
   butter or margarine,
   softened
¼ cup peanut butter,
   preferably chunk style
½ cup brown sugar
1 egg
½ cup molasses
½ milk

1 cup white flour
1 cup whole wheat flour
1½ teaspoons baking powder
¼ teaspoon salt
½ teaspoon cinnamon
¼ teaspoon baking soda
1½ cups chopped ripe
   banana
½ cup raisins

1. In a bowl, cream the butter or margarine and peanut butter with the brown sugar. Beat in the egg, then the molasses and milk.
2. In another bowl, stir together the flours, baking powder, salt, cinnamon, and baking soda. Beat into the peanut butter mixture. Stir in the banana pieces and raisins.
3. Spread the batter into a greased and floured 16" x 11" jelly roll pan (batter will be thin). Bake in a 350° oven for 25 to 30 minutes, or until a toothpick inserted in the center comes out clean. Let cool on a rack; and when cool, cut into bars.

YIELD: 24 2-inch x 4-inch bars

GRANDMOTHER'S JAM SQUARES

My grandmother has been making these jam bars for as long as I can remember; and the buttery-rich squares are popular with all her friends and relatives. She uses apricot or strawberry jam, but you may really use any favorite flavor jam or preserves (don't use jelly, as the consistency is different). The bars are in two layers—a rich butter-and-egg-yolk bottom covered with jam and a light, spiced meringue on top.

Meringue Topping:
2 egg whites
½ cup granulated sugar
¼ teaspoon cinnamon

½ cup finely chopped
    walnuts

Bottom Layer:
½ cup (1 stick) butter,
    softened (use real butter, if
    possible)
½ cup confectioners' sugar

2 egg yolks
1 cup flour
⅔ cup jam

1. Beat the egg whites until stiff. Gradually beat in the granulated sugar until the whites are glossy. Beat in the cinnamon and walnuts. Set aside.
2. In a bowl, cream the butter with the confectioners' sugar. Beat in the egg yolks, then the flour. Pat into a well-greased and floured 8" x 8" pan. Bake in a 350° oven for 12 minutes.
3. Spread the bottom layer with the jam and then with the meringue topping. Bake the bars 30 minutes longer. Let cool on a rack and then cut into squares.

YIELD: 36 1½-inch squares

HONEY BRAN JAM BARS

Honey and bran make for a wholesome crust in a most delightful bar that's perfect for lunch-box treats. Here's an opportunity to use up those jars of jam that vie for space in the refrigerator; you can even use several different flavors if you like, confining each to an area of the baking pan. Any favorite jam will work well in this recipe; I like the tangy, rather unusual taste of plum jam.

½ cup (1 stick) butter or
   margarine, softened
⅓ cup brown sugar
½ cup honey
1 egg
1 teaspoon vanilla
1 cup bran cereal, such as
   All-Bran

1 cup white flour
1 cup whole wheat flour
¼ teaspoon baking soda
¼ teaspoon salt
½ cup jam

1. In a bowl, cream the butter or margarine with the brown sugar and honey. Beat in the egg and vanilla.
2. In another bowl, stir together the bran, flours, baking soda, and salt. Beat into the creamed mixture.
3. Spread half the batter evenly in a greased and floured 8" x 10" baking pan. Spread with jam and then with the rest of the batter. (You may find it easiest to drop the batter over the jam in tiny spoonfuls and then spread it with a knife; it's okay if a little jam pokes through the batter.) Bake the bars in a 375° oven for 25 minutes, or until a toothpick inserted into the top layer comes out clean (if you put the toothpick into the jam, it will become sticky). Let cool on a rack and then cut into squares.

YIELD: 20 2-inch bars

ZUCCHINI RAISIN BARS

With zucchini breads and cakes becoming ever increasingly popular, why not zucchini bars, too? These are delectably chewy, with a wholesome bran flavor and plenty of raisins and coconut in each bite.

2 eggs
1 cup brown sugar
½ cup (1 stick) butter or
  margarine, melted
1 tablespoon water
1 teaspoon vanilla
1 cup white flour
1 cup whole wheat flour
¼ teaspoon nutmeg

¼ teaspoon salt
1 teaspoon baking soda
1½ cups bran cereal, such as
  All-Bran
½ cup dark raisins
½ cup golden raisins
1 cup shredded coconut
3 cups coarsely grated
  zucchini

1. In a large bowl, beat the eggs. Gradually beat in the brown sugar. When done, the mixture should be thick and pale. Beat in the melted butter or margarine, water, and vanilla.
2. In another bowl, stir together the flours, nutmeg, salt, baking soda, and bran. Beat into the liquid mixture, then stir in the raisins, coconut, and zucchini.
3. Turn the batter into a greased and floured 9" x 13" baking pan. Bake the bars in a 350° oven for 40 minutes, or until a toothpick inserted in the center comes out clean. Let cool on a rack and then cut into bars.

YIELD: 24 2-inch bars

SWEET POTATO BARS

Mashed sweet potatoes lend an attractive orange color to these especially hearty and nutritious spice bars.

1 egg
⅓ cup granulated sugar
⅓ cup brown sugar
½ cup (1 stick) butter or
   margarine, melted
½ cup mashed cooked sweet
   potatoes
¾ cup milk
½ teaspoon vanilla
1½ cups whole wheat flour

½ teaspoon baking powder
¼ teaspoon baking soda
¼ teaspoon salt
½ teaspoon cinnamon
1½ cups rolled oats
1 cup bran cereal, such as
   All-Bran
¼ cup finely chopped
   walnuts
½ cup raisins

---

1. In a large bowl, beat the egg with the sugars until the mixture is thick. Beat in the melted butter or margarine, then the sweet potatoes, milk, and vanilla.
2. In another bowl, stir together the whole wheat flour, baking powder, baking soda, salt, cinnamon, oats, and bran. Beat into the sweet potato mixture and then stir in the walnuts and raisins.
3. Spread the batter evenly in a greased and floured 8″ x 8″ pan. Bake the bars in a 375° oven for 35 minutes, or until a toothpick inserted in the center comes out clean. Let cool on a rack and then cut into bars.

YIELD: 16 2-inch bars

SPICED SQUASH BARS

Mashed winter squash lends a deep orange color to these quickly made, moist spice bars. You may use freshly cooked and pureed squash (see page 83), thawed frozen mashed squash, or canned solid-pack pumpkin in this recipe.

2 eggs
1 cup sugar
¼ cup salad oil
¼ cup yogurt
1 cup cooked, pureed
   winter squash
1 teaspoon vanilla

1¼ cups flour
1 teaspoon baking powder
½ teaspoon baking soda
2 teaspoons cinnamon
1 teaspoon ginger
½ teaspoon nutmeg
¼ teaspoon salt

1. In a bowl, beat the eggs. Gradually beat in the sugar until the mixture is thick. Beat in the oil, yogurt, squash, and vanilla.
2. In another bowl, stir together the flour, baking powder, baking soda, spices, and salt. Beat into the squash mixture.
3. Turn the batter into a greased and floured 8" x 10" baking pan. Bake the bars in a 375° oven for about 25 minutes, or until a toothpick inserted in the center comes out clean. Let cool on a rack; and when cool, cut into bars.

YIELD: 16 2-inch by 2½-inch bars

PEANUT BUTTER FRUIT BARS

Here's another peanut butter bar recipe, this one filled with fresh apples and pears. The bars are very moist and quite delicate, so they're best eaten with a fork.

⅓ cup (5⅓ tablespoons) butter or margarine, softened
⅓ cup peanut butter, preferably chunk style
⅓ cup granulated sugar
⅓ cup brown sugar
1 egg
¾ cup flour

¼ teaspoon baking powder
½ teaspoon baking soda
¼ teaspoon salt
3 pears, peeled, cored, and diced
2 apples, peeled, cored, and diced

1. In a bowl, cream the butter or margarine with the peanut butter and sugars. Beat in the egg.
2. In another bowl, stir together the flour, baking powder, baking soda, and salt. Beat into the peanut butter mixture and then stir in the pears and apples.
3. Turn the batter into a greased and floured 8" x 10" baking pan and spread it evenly. Bake the bars in a 350° oven for 35 minutes, or until they test done with a toothpick (since these bars are quite moist, the toothpick will be almost, but not completely, clean). Transfer to a rack to cool; then cut into bars. NOTE: Because these are so moist and fruity, they are best stored in the refrigerator.

YIELD: 12 2-inch by 3-inch bars

GERMAN CHRISTMAS BARS

Candied cherries enhance these chewy spice bars that pack and keep well for gift-giving during the holidays. As the bars are very thin, they bake quickly. This recipe makes two pans, but you may cut all measurements in half for one pan, if desired.

2 eggs	½ teaspoon baking soda
¾ cup brown sugar	1 teaspoon cinnamon
1 cup dark corn syrup	½ teaspoon ground cloves
1 tablespoon lemon juice	½ teaspoon nutmeg
2¼ cups flour	1 cup diced candied
½ cup cornstarch	cherries

1. In a large bowl, beat the eggs. Gradually beat in the brown sugar until the mixture is thick. Beat in the corn syrup and lemon juice.
2. In another bowl, stir together the flour, cornstarch, baking soda, and spices. Beat into the egg mixture, and then stir in the cherries.
3. Divide the batter between 2 greased and floured 11" x 16" jelly roll pans, and spread it evenly.
4. Bake the bars in a 400° oven for 12 to 15 minutes, or until golden and a toothpick inserted in the center comes out clean. When cool, cut into squares.

YIELD: 48 2-inch bars

TOMATO SOUP OATMEAL BARS

Like the tomato soup cake recipe in the spice cake chapter, this bar recipe sounds strange but tastes surprisingly delicious. Tomato soup adds body to these hearty, spicy oatmeal bars.

¾ cup (1½ sticks) butter or margarine, softened
1 cup brown sugar
⅓ cup granulated sugar
1 egg
1 can (10¾ ounces) condensed tomato soup
1½ cups flour

1 teaspoon baking powder
½ teaspoon baking soda
2 teaspoons cinnamon
1 teaspoon nutmeg
2 cups rolled oats
½ cup raisins
½ cup coarsely chopped walnuts

1. In a large bowl, cream the butter or margarine with the sugars. Beat in the egg, then the tomato soup.
2. In another bowl, stir together the flour, baking powder, baking soda, spices, and oats. Beat into the tomato mixture and then stir in the raisins and walnuts.
3. Spread the batter evenly in a greased and floured 9" x 13" baking pan. Bake the bars in a 350° oven for 30 minutes, or until a toothpick inserted in the center comes out clean. Transfer to a rack to cool and then cut into bars.

YIELD: 24 2-inch bars

RAISIN NUT SPICE BARS

Molasses, raisins, nuts, and a variety of spices go into these chewy, tantalizing bars that keep well for lunch-box treats or mailing. These are delicious warm or cooled, so enjoy one right from the oven, as their fragrance can't be resisted easily.

½ cup (1 stick) butter or
   margarine, softened
½ cup sugar
2 eggs
½ cup molasses
1 cup white flour
1 cup whole wheat flour
2 teaspoons baking powder
¼ teaspoon baking soda

1½ teaspoons cinnamon
½ teaspoon ground cloves
½ teaspoon ginger
¼ teaspoon nutmeg
¼ teaspoon salt
½ cup raisins
½ cup coarsely chopped
   walnuts

---

1. In a bowl, cream the butter or margarine with the sugar. Beat in the eggs, then the molasses.
2. In another bowl, stir together the flours, baking powder, baking soda, spices, and salt. Beat into the creamed mixture and stir in the raisins and walnuts.
3. Spread the batter evenly in a greased and floured 9" x 13" baking pan. Bake the bars in a 350° oven for 25 minutes, or until a toothpick inserted in the center comes out clean. Let cool on a rack and then cut into bars.

YIELD: 24 2-inch bars

HEALTH BARS

Peanut butter, wheat germ, whole wheat flour, and oats all go into these nutritious snack bars that are flecked with chocolate chips. They'll become everyone's lunch-box favorites.

6 tablespoons (¾ stick) butter
  or margarine, softened
½ cup peanut butter,
  preferably chunk style
1 cup brown sugar
1 egg
1 teaspoon vanilla

1¼ cups whole wheat flour
½ cup wheat germ
1 cup rolled oats
½ teaspoon baking soda
¼ teaspoon salt
½ cup (3 ounces) semisweet
  chocolate morsels

---

1. In a bowl, cream the butter and peanut butter with the brown sugar. Beat in the egg and vanilla.
2. In another bowl, stir together the flour, wheat germ, oats, baking soda, and salt. Beat into the creamed mixture and then stir in the chocolate morsels.
3. Spread the batter evenly in a greased and floured 9" x 13" baking pan. Bake the bars in a 375° oven for about 15 minutes, or until a toothpick inserted in the center comes out clean. Let cool on a rack, then cut into bars.

YIELD: 24 2-inch bars

COCONUT RUM FRUIT BARS

Dried prunes and apricots are soaked in coconut rum liqueur before being folded into a batter that becomes crumbly rich oatmeal bars.

¼ cup diced pitted dried prunes
½ cup diced apricots
⅓ cup coconut rum liqueur
½ cup (1 stick) butter or margarine, softened
¾ cup brown sugar
2 eggs

1 teaspoon vanilla
1 cup flour
1 teaspoon baking powder
½ teaspoon baking soda
¼ teaspoon salt
1 cup rolled oats
¼ cup finely chopped walnuts

1. In a small bowl, combine the prunes, apricots, and coconut rum liqueur. Let sit at least 30 minutes.
2. In a bowl, cream the butter or margarine with the brown sugar. Beat in the eggs and vanilla.
3. In another bowl, stir together the flour, baking powder, baking soda, salt, and rolled oats. Beat into the creamed mixture and then stir in the walnuts, dried fruits, and any unabsorbed liqueur.
4. Turn the batter into a greased and floured 9" x 13" baking pan. Bake the bars in a 350° oven for 30 minutes, or until they test done with a toothpick (because these bars are quite moist, the toothpick will be almost, but not completely, clean). Let cool on a rack and then cut into bars.

YIELD: 24 2-inch bars

SOUTHERN CORNMEAL BARS

Because these bars contain cornmeal rather than flour, they are very crumbly. But they're also wonderfully flavored with pecans and coconut, and rich with butter. The cornmeal lends a pleasing heartiness and wholesome good taste.

2 eggs	¾ cup cornmeal
1 cup brown sugar	½ teaspoon baking powder
½ cup (1 stick) butter, melted	1 cup flaked coconut
(use real butter, if possible)	⅔ cup chopped pecans

1. In a bowl, beat the eggs. Gradually beat in the brown sugar. When done, the mixture should be thick. Beat in the melted butter, then the cornmeal and baking powder. Stir in the coconut and pecans.
2. Turn the batter into a greased and floured 8" x 8" pan. Bake the bars in a 350° oven for 30 minutes, or until they test done with a toothpick (because these bars are so moist, the toothpick will be almost, but not completely, clean). Let cool on a rack, then cut into bars.

YIELD: 16 2-inch bars

"Quick" Or Tea Breads

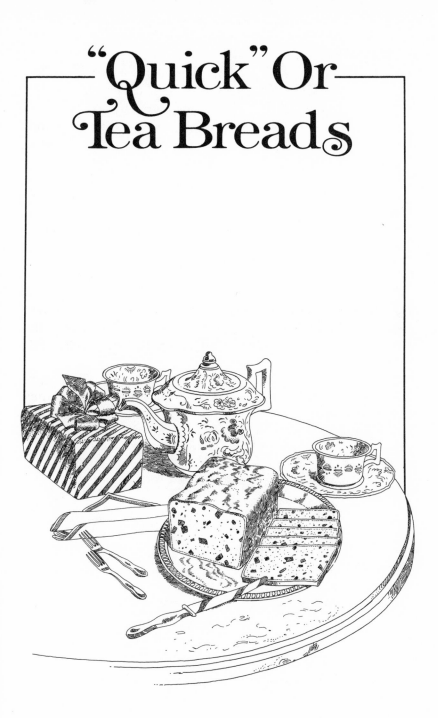

Although these are classified as breads, they are prepared by the same rules as for cakes and so certainly deserve a place in this book. Perhaps the main difference is that "quick" breads are somewhat less sweet than the more traditional dessert cakes.

Tea breads can be served almost any time you would ordinarily want a piece of cake. For lunch-box treats, between-meal snacks, or family desserts along with a fruit salad, these are ideal. Many people also enjoy sandwiching together two thin slices from a loaf of banana, carrot, date, or nut bread with cream cheese as part of a fancy lunch. Quick breads are also an easy way to make any breakfast or brunch more appealing.

Many of my "quick" breads are made with at least fifty percent whole wheat flour. This produces a denser texture, heartier flavor, and contributes to their "breadiness."

CRANBERRY SAUCE LOAF

Here's another cranberry loaf that's welcome on any holiday table. This version is made with canned cranberry sauce and so is especially quick and easy to whip up.

6 tablespoons (¾ stick) butter or margarine, softened
¾ cup brown sugar
2 eggs
1 cup (1 8-ounce can or half of 1 16-ounce can) whole-berry cranberry sauce

¾ cup white flour
¾ cup whole wheat flour
1 teaspoon baking powder
1 teaspoon baking soda
1 teaspoon cinnamon
¼ teaspoon ground cloves
⅓ cup finely chopped walnuts
⅓ cup raisins

1. In a bowl, cream the butter or margarine with the brown sugar. Beat in the eggs, then the cranberry sauce.
2. In another bowl, stir together the flours, baking powder, baking soda, and spices. Beat into the cranberry mixture and then stir in the walnuts and raisins.
3. Turn the batter into a greased and floured 9" x 5" loaf pan. Bake the bread in a 350° oven for 1 hour, or until it tests done with a toothpick. Let pan cool on a rack before removing bread.

YIELD: 8 to 10 slices

CRANBERRY–ORANGE BREAD

This is the classic cranberry bread, with a sweet orange batter to complement the tart berries; I have been making it for Thanksgiving dinner since I was twelve years old. The cranberries should be coarsely chopped so their juices permeate the loaf. This is most easily done by mixing the batter in a food processor or blender. If you don't have one of these appliances, though, you will have to resort to the chopper or knife.

4 tablespoons (½ stick) butter or margarine, softened
1 cup sugar
1 egg
1 tablespoon grated orange rind

¾ cup orange juice
1½ cups cranberries
½ cup walnuts
1 cup white flour
1 cup whole wheat flour
1½ teaspoons baking soda
¼ teaspoon salt

Instructions for food processor:
1. With the steel blade in place, process the butter or margarine with the sugar and ungrated orange rind (removed from

1 orange with a vegetable peeler) until sugar is incorporated into the butter and the rind is very finely chopped. Add the egg and orange juice and process until incorporated. Add the cranberries and walnuts and process until coarsely chopped. Add all remaining ingredients and process with quick on-off movements until they are just blended into the rest of the batter.

Instructions for blender:

1. Place the butter or margarine, sugar, egg, ungrated orange rind (removed from 1 orange with a vegetable peeler), and orange juice in a blender and blend until the orange peel is finely chopped. Add the cranberries and walnuts and blend until they are coarsely chopped. Stir together the remaining ingredients in a bowl and stir in the contents of the blender.

Instructions for electric mixer:

1. Cream the butter or margarine with the sugar in a bowl. Beat in the egg, then the grated orange rind and orange juice. In another bowl, stir together the dry ingredients. Beat these into the creamed mixture and then stir in the chopped cranberries and walnuts.

To Bake:

2. Turn the batter into a greased and floured 9" x 5" loaf pan. Bake the loaf in a 350° oven for about 1 hour, or until it tests done with a toothpick. Transfer pan to a rack to cool before removing bread.

YIELD: 8 to 10 slices

BANANA NUT BREAD

Here's a traditional favorite, a simple, hearty banana bread that's dotted with crunchy walnuts. Plain or spread with cream cheese, this is always a sure winner.

½ cup (1 stick) butter or margarine, softened
⅔ cup sugar
2 eggs
¼ cup yogurt
1¼ cups mashed ripe bananas
1 cup white flour
1 cup whole wheat flour
1½ teaspoon baking powder
½ teaspoon baking soda
1 teaspoon cinnamon
⅛ teaspoon cardamon
¼ teaspoon salt
⅔ cup coarsely chopped walnuts

1. In a bowl, cream the butter or margarine with the sugar. Beat in the eggs, then the yogurt and mashed bananas.
2. In another bowl, stir together the flours, baking powder, baking soda, spices, and salt. Beat into the banana mixture and then stir in the walnuts.
3. Turn the batter into a greased and floured 9" x 5" loaf pan. Bake the bread in a 350° oven for 1 hour, or until it tests done with a toothpick. Transfer pan to a rack to cool before removing bread.

YIELD: 8 to 10 slices

BLUEBERRY–BANANA BREAD

Ripe blueberries make this tender banana bread especially moist and attractive. It's particularly pleasing at breakfast, spread with butter or cream cheese.

⅓ cup (5⅓ tablespoons) butter
   or margarine, softened
⅓ cup granulated sugar
⅓ cup brown sugar
2 eggs
1 cup mashed ripe bananas
¾ cup white flour

¾ cup whole wheat flour
½ cup rolled oats
2 teaspoons baking powder
¼ teaspoon salt
1 cup blueberries
½ cup finely chopped
   walnuts

---

1. In a bowl, cream the butter or margarine with the sugars. Beat in the eggs, then the bananas.
2. In another bowl, stir together the flours, oats, baking powder, and salt. Beat into the banana mixture and then stir in the blueberries and walnuts.
3. Turn the batter into a greased and floured 9" x 5" loaf pan. Bake the bread in a 350° oven for 1 hour, or until it tests done with a toothpick. Let pan cool on a rack before removing bread.

YIELD: 8 to 10 slices

BANANA–CARROT BREAD

*Two favorites team up in this hearty, healthful, and color-
ful loaf. Use it for tea sandwiches filled with cream cheese
or as a between meal or lunch-box snack.*

4 tablespoons (½ stick)
   butter or margarine,
   softened
½ cup sugar
2 eggs
1 cup mashed ripe bananas
1 teaspoon vanilla
1 cup grated carrots
1 cup white flour

1 cup whole wheat flour
2 teaspoons baking powder
¼ teaspoon baking soda
½ teaspoon cinnamon
⅛ teaspoon ground cloves
¼ teaspoon salt
½ cup coarsely chopped
   walnuts

1. In a large bowl, cream the butter or margarine with the
   sugar. Beat in the eggs, then the bananas, vanilla, and carrots.
2. In another bowl, stir together the flours, baking powder,
   baking soda, spices, and salt. Beat into the creamed mixture and then stir in the walnuts.
3. Turn the batter into a greased and floured 9" x 13" loaf
   pan. Bake the bread in a 350° oven for 65 to 70 minutes, or
   until it tests done with a toothpick. Transfer to a rack to
   cool before removing from the pan.

YIELD: 8 servings

LEMON BREAD, WITH VARIATION

This bread is so refreshingly tart and tangy tasting, you'll find yourself serving it again and again. The bread is also quite economical. It goes well as a between-meal snack, with a salad lunch, or with a fresh fruit dessert.

⅓ cup (5⅓ tablespoons) butter or margarine, softened
1 cup sugar
2 eggs
1 tablespoon grated lemon rind

1 cup milk
1 cup white flour
1 cup whole wheat flour
¼ teaspoon salt
1 tablespoon baking powder

---

1. In a bowl, cream the butter or margarine with the sugar. Beat in the eggs, then the lemon rind and milk.
2. In another bowl, stir together the flours, salt, and baking powder. Beat into the creamed mixture.
3. Turn the batter into a greased and floured 9" x 5" loaf pan. Bake the bread in a 325° oven for about 1 hour, or until it tests done with a toothpick. Let pan cool on a rack before removing bread.

YIELD: 8 to 10 slices

Cranberry–Lemon Bread (great for Thanksgiving!): Add 1½ cups coarsely chopped cranberries to the batter after mixing in the dry ingredients.

FRESH STRAWBERRY BREAD

Here's a bread for a springtime luncheon. Serve it with a fruit or chicken salad, plain or sandwiched with cream cheese. Fresh strawberries fill the loaf with pretty pink tints and a delectable fruity taste.

NOTE: *If possible, toss the sugar with the berries a day in advance; this will draw out the juices, making the bread even more flavorful.*

1 cup sliced strawberries
1 cup sugar, divided usage
2 eggs
½ cup (1 stick) butter or
   margarine, melted
¾ cup white flour

¾ cup whole wheat flour
½ teaspoon baking soda
¼ teaspoon salt
1½ teaspoons cinnamon
½ cup finely chopped
   walnuts

1. Toss the strawberries with ½ cup sugar. Let stand at room temperature 1 hour or in the refrigerator overnight.
2. In a bowl, beat the eggs. Gradually beat in the remaining ½ cup sugar. Then beat in the melted butter or margarine and any syrup that forms around the berries.
3. In another bowl, mix together the flours, baking soda, salt, and cinnamon. Beat into the liquid mixture and then gently stir in the strawberries and walnuts.
4. Turn the batter into a greased and floured 9" x 5" loaf pan. Bake in a 350° oven for 50 minutes, or until it tests done with a toothpick. Transfer pan to a rack to cool before removing bread.

YIELD: 8 to 10 slices

CHERRY BREAD

Each slice of this delightful bread is filled with rounds of dark, delicious cherries. Although it is tedious to pit fresh cherries (unless you have a cherry pitter), the taste is better than that of the canned fruit. However, if you are in the mood for this bread and fresh cherries are unavailable or too much of a bother, by all means substitute the canned dark sweet variety.

2 eggs
1 cup sugar
4 tablespoons (½ stick) butter or margarine, melted
grated rind of 1 lemon
½ cup apple juice
¾ cup white flour

¾ cup whole wheat flour
½ teaspoon baking powder
½ teaspoon baking soda
¼ teaspoon salt
1⅓ cups pitted dark sweet cherries, such as Bing
½ cup coarsely chopped walnuts

1. In a bowl, beat the eggs. Gradually beat in the sugar. When done, the mixture should be thick and pale. Beat in the melted butter or margarine, then the lemon rind and apple juice.
2. In another bowl, stir together the flours, baking powder, baking soda, and salt. Beat into the liquid ingredients and then gently stir in the cherries and walnuts.
3. Turn the batter into a greased and floured 9" x 5" loaf pan. Bake the bread in a 350° oven for 45 minutes, or until it tests done with a toothpick. Transfer pan to a rack to cool before removing bread.

YIELD: 8 to 10 slices

PLUMMY OATMEAL BREAD

Fresh purple plums and chewy rolled oats make this an especially delightful bread. It's wonderful for brunch spread with whipped cream cheese and is also a most pleasant snack with coffee or tea.

2 eggs
¾ cup sugar
4 tablespoons (½ stick)
   butter or margarine, melted
1 cup milk
1 cup white flour
1 cup whole wheat flour
1 tablespoon baking powder

½ teaspoon baking soda
¼ teaspoon salt
½ teaspoon cinnamon
1 cup rolled oats
1 cup diced purple plums,
   preferably Italian prune
   plums

1. In a bowl, beat the eggs. Gradually beat in the sugar; when done, the mixture should be thick and pale. Beat in the melted butter or margarine and then the milk.
2. In another bowl, stir together the flours, baking powder, baking soda, salt, cinnamon, and oats. Beat into the liquid mixture and then stir in the plums.
3. Turn the batter into a greased and floured 9" x 5" loaf pan. Bake the bread in a 350° oven for 1 hour, or until it tests done with a toothpick. Let pan cool on a rack before removing bread.

YIELD: 8 to 10 slices

PUMPKIN WHEAT RING

Shredded wheat cereal gives this moist, tender loaf a refreshing hearty quality. The bread is baked in a tube pan, so it's ideal for a brunch crowd. If you prefer, though, you may substitute two 9" x 5" loaf pans and reserve one bread for another occasion. NOTE: *For information on preparing fresh pumpkin for baking, see page 83. The shredded wheat should be finely crushed for this recipe. This is most easily done with the steel blade of a food processor; but if you lack this appliance, you can roll it between two pieces of wax paper with a rolling pin.*

3 eggs
1¼ cups brown sugar
¾ cup (1½ sticks) butter or
   margarine, melted
1 cup pumpkin puree
   (homemade, or canned
   solid-pack pumpkin)
¾ cup milk
1½ cups white flour
1½ cups whole wheat flour

¼ teaspoon salt
2 teaspoons baking powder
2 teaspoons cinnamon
3 large shredded wheat
   biscuits, finely rolled or
   crushed in a food
   processor (about ¾ cups)
1 cup coarsely chopped
   walnuts
1 cup diced dates

1. In a large bowl, beat the eggs. Gradually beat in the brown sugar until the mixture is thick. Beat in the melted butter or margarine, then the pumpkin and milk.
2. In another bowl, stir together the flours, salt, baking powder, and cinnamon. Beat into the pumpkin mixture and then stir in the shredded wheat, walnuts, and dates.
3. Turn the batter into a greased and floured tube pan. Bake in a 350° oven for 1 hour, or until a toothpick inserted in the bread comes out clean. Let pan cool on a rack before removing bread.

YIELD: 20 slices

SPICED PUMPKIN LOAF

Cocoa becomes a spice in this aromatic pumpkin loaf that's also flavored with cinnamon, ginger, and cloves. It's an ideal holiday bread—for gift-giving or for your own table. For information on preparing fresh pumpkin for cakes and breads, see page 83.

6 tablespoons (¾ stick) butter or margarine, softened
1 cup brown sugar
2 eggs
1 cup pumpkin puree (homemade, or canned solid-pack pumpkin)
¼ cup milk
1 cup white flour
1 cup whole wheat flour

2 teaspoons baking powder
2 teaspoons cocoa, sifted if lumpy
1 teaspoon cinnamon
½ teaspoon ginger
¼ teaspoon ground cloves
¼ teaspoon salt
¼ teaspoon baking soda
½ cup coarsely chopped walnuts

1. In a bowl, cream the butter or margarine with the brown sugar. Beat in the eggs, then the pumpkin puree and milk.
2. In another bowl, stir together the flours, baking powder, cocoa, spices, salt, and baking soda. Beat into the pumpkin mixture and then stir in the walnuts.
3. Turn the batter into a greased and floured 9" x 5" loaf pan. Bake the bread in a 350° oven for about 1 hour, or until it tests done with a toothpick. Transfer pan to a rack to cool before removing bread.

YIELD: 8 to 10 slices

PUMPKIN MOLASSES BREAD

Here's yet another pumpkin bread, this one dark and well-flavored with molasses and plenty of spices. For information on preparing fresh pumpkin for baking, see page 83.

⅓ cup raisins
⅓ cup hot tap water
⅓ cup (5⅓ tablespoons)
   butter or margarine,
   softened
1 cup sugar
⅓ cup molasses
2 eggs
1 cup pumpkin puree
   (homemade, or canned
   solid-pack pumpkin)

¾ cup white flour
¾ cup whole wheat flour
2½ tablespoons wheat germ
½ teaspoon cinnamon
¼ teaspoon ground cloves
¼ teaspoon nutmeg
¼ teaspoon baking powder
½ teaspoon baking soda
¼ teaspoon salt
⅓ cup chopped walnuts

-----

1. Pour the hot water over the raisins and let sit while preparing the rest of batter.
2. In a large bowl, cream the butter or margarine with the sugar and molasses. Beat in the eggs, then the pumpkin puree.
3. In another bowl, stir together the flours, wheat germ, spices, baking powder, baking soda, and salt. Beat into the pumpkin mixture, then stir in the walnuts and the raisins plus any water that was not absorbed.
4. Turn the batter into a greased and floured 9" x 5" loaf pan. Bake the bread in a 350° oven for about 65 minutes, or until a toothpick inserted into it comes out clean. Let pan cool on a rack before removing bread.

YIELD: 8 to 10 slices

MARINATED PRUNE BREAD

Dry sherry, which is mostly absorbed by the prunes, makes this a delightfully different loaf. NOTE: *It's best to marinate the prunes a day in advance, but an hour will do if you are pressed for time.*

1 cup finely chopped pitted
   dried prunes
¼ cup dry sherry
2 eggs
½ cup sugar
1 cup milk

1 cup white flour
1 cup whole wheat flour
1 tablespoon baking powder
¼ teaspoon salt
½ teaspoon cinnamon

1. Stir together the prunes and sherry in a bowl. Cover and let sit from 1 hour to overnight.
2. In a bowl, beat the eggs. Gradually beat in the sugar. When done, the mixture should be thick and pale. Beat in the milk.
3. In another bowl, stir together the flours, baking powder, salt, and cinnamon. Beat into the liquid mixture, then stir in the prunes, along with any unabsorbed sherry.
4. Turn the batter into a greased and floured 9" x 5" loaf pan. Bake the bread in a 350° oven for 50 to 60 minutes, or until it tests done with a toothpick. Transfer pan to a rack to cool before removing bread.

YIELD: 8 to 10 slices

GRANDMOTHER'S DATE AND NUT BREAD

This is my grandmother's recipe, which she always makes in two-loaf batches because it's so popular. The bread isn't terribly rich, and the liquid used to soak the dates goes into the batter, giving it even more of a date flavor. The bread is delicious as a dessert or between-meal snack, or spread with cream cheese for teatime sandwiches.

1 8-ounce package pitted dates, chopped coarsely	2 cups boiling water
½ cup raisins	2 eggs
3 tablespoons butter or margarine, softened	1½ cups sugar
	1 teaspoon vanilla
2 teaspoons baking soda	1 cup whole wheat flour
2 teaspoons freeze-dried coffee or 2½ teaspoons instant coffee powder	3 cups white flour
	½ teaspoon cinnamon
	1 cup coarsely chopped walnuts

1. In a bowl, stir together the dates, raisins, butter or margarine, baking soda, coffee, and water. Let sit until lukewarm and drain well, reserving the liquid.
2. In a large bowl, beat the eggs. Gradually beat in the sugar until the mixture is thick and pale. Beat in the date liquid and vanilla.
3. In another bowl, stir together the flours and cinnamon. Beat into the liquid mixture and then stir in the dates, raisins, and walnuts.
4. Turn the batter into 2 greased and floured 9" x 5" loaf pans. Bake the loaves in a 350° oven for about 1 hour, or until they test done with a toothpick. Transfer pans to a rack to cool before removing breads. NOTE: These freeze very well; or eat one loaf and give the other as a gift.

YIELD: 2 loaves, 8 slices each

BRITISH TEA LOAF

Here's a pleasant spiced loaf from Somerset, England, that's sweetened with honey and so keeps very well. Because it contains no butter or margarine, it's not at all rich. However, the

British serve the bread thickly spread with butter to compensate. Whatever way you choose to serve it, though—buttered
or plain—it makes a great between-meal snack.

1 egg
½ cup brown sugar
¾ cup honey
⅓ cup milk
1¼ cups white flour
1¼ cups whole wheat flour
1 teaspoon ginger

½ teaspoon ground cloves
½ teaspoon cinnamon
1 teaspoon baking soda
⅓ cup diced candied orange
  peel
⅓ cup raisins

---

1. In a bowl, beat the egg and brown sugar together very well.
   Beat in the honey, then the milk.
2. In another bowl, stir together the flours, spices, and baking soda. Beat into the liquid mixture and then stir in the
   orange peel and raisins.
3. Turn the batter into a greased and floured 9" x 5" loaf
   pan. Bake the bread in a 300° oven for 65 minutes, or until
   it tests done with the toothpick. Let pan cool on a rack
   before removing bread. Serve with butter if desired.

YIELD: 8 to 10 slices

PEANUT BUTTER RAISIN BREAD

Raisins fleck this most peanutty peanut butter bread that's
perfect for adults and children alike who are addicted to this
flavor.

2½ tablespoons butter or
  margarine, softened
1 cup minus 2 tablespoons
  peanut butter, preferably
  chunk style
¾ cup sugar
2 eggs

1¼ cups milk
1 cup plus 2 tablespoons
  white flour
1 cup whole wheat flour
2½ teaspoons baking powder
¼ teaspoon salt
¾ cup raisins

1. In a bowl, cream the butter or margarine and peanut butter with the sugar. Beat in the eggs, then the milk.
2. In another bowl, stir together the flours, baking powder,
   and salt. Beat into the peanut mixture and then stir in the
   raisins.
3. Turn the batter into a greased and floured 9" x 5" loaf
   pan. Bake the bread in a 350° oven for 1 hour, or until it
   tests done with a toothpick. Let pan cool on a rack before
   removing the bread.
YIELD: 8 to 10 slices

JASMINE TEA BREAD

Flower-scented jasmine tea, as well as the grated rind of
lemon, lime, and orange, make for an exotic-tasting loaf.

4 tablespoons (½ stick)
  butter or margarine,
  softened
¾ cup brown sugar
1 egg
1 teaspoon grated lemon
  rind
1 teaspoon grated lime rind
1 tablespoon grated orange
  rind
¾ cup orange juice

½ cup brewed jasmine tea
1½ cups white flour
1½ cups whole wheat flour
¼ teaspoon salt
¼ teaspoon ginger
¼ teaspoon cinnamon
1 teaspoon baking powder
1 teaspoon baking soda
½ cup slivered blanched
  almonds

1. In a bowl, cream the butter or margarine with the brown
   sugar. Beat in the egg, then the grated rinds, orange juice,
   and tea.
2. In another bowl, stir together the flours, salt, spices, baking powder, and baking soda. Beat into the creamed mixture and then stir in the almonds.

3. Turn the batter into a greased and floured 9" x 5" loaf pan. Bake the bread in a 350° oven for 50 minutes, or until it tests done with a toothpick. Transfer pan to a rack to cool before removing bread.

YIELD: 8 to 10 slices

HEALTH BREAD

Cottage cheese, yogurt, raisins, and walnuts make this an especially healthful loaf. Tastewise, it's most appealing, too.

⅓ cup (5⅓ tablespoons) butter or margarine, softened
½ cup brown sugar
1 egg
1 tablespoon grated orange rind
½ cup cottage cheese
½ cup yogurt
⅓ cup orange juice

1 cup white flour
1 cup whole wheat flour
½ teaspoon cinnamon
¼ teaspoon nutmeg
2 teaspoons baking powder
½ teaspoon baking soda
1½ cups raisins
⅓ cup coarsely chopped walnuts

1. In a bowl, cream the butter or margarine with the brown sugar. Beat in the egg, then the orange rind, cottage cheese, yogurt, and orange juice.
2. In another bowl, stir together the flours, cinnamon, nutmeg, baking powder, and baking soda. Beat into the creamed mixture and then stir in the raisins and nuts.
3. Turn the batter into a greased and floured 9" x 5" loaf pan. Bake the bread in a 350° oven for 1 hour, or until it tests done with a toothpick. Let the pan cool on a rack before removing the bread.

YIELD: 8 to 10 slices

GRAPE NUT BREAD

Hearty Grape Nuts cereal lends a pleasant texture and wholesome good flavor to this honey-sweetened loaf.

4 tablespoons (½ stick)
  butter or margarine,
  softened
½ cup honey
2 eggs
½ teaspoon vanilla
¾ cup milk

1 cup white flour
1 cup plus 2 tablespoons
  whole wheat flour
2 teaspoons baking powder
¼ teaspoon salt
¾ cup Grape Nuts cereal

---

1. In a bowl, cream the butter or margarine with the honey. Beat in the eggs, then the vanilla and milk.
2. In another bowl, stir together the flours, baking powder, and salt. Beat into the creamed mixture and then stir in the Grape Nuts.
3. Turn the batter into a greased and floured 9" x 5" loaf pan. Bake the bread in a 325° oven for 50 minutes, or until it tests done with a toothpick. Transfer pan to a rack to cool before removing bread.

YIELD: 8 to 10 slices

PINEAPPLE–ZUCCHINI LOAF

Zucchini breads have swept the country in the last decade. At first probably an experimental result of someone's bumper zucchini crop, now they are enjoyed purely for their rich, good taste. This version, filled with fruity pineapple, is sweet enough to serve for dessert with a fresh fruit salad. It's very moist, so it keeps well for days in the refrigerator. The recipe makes two loaves; give one away as a gift, or freeze it for later use.

3 eggs
2 cups sugar
1 cup (2 sticks) butter or
  margarine, melted
1½ cups white flour
1½ cups whole wheat flour
2 teaspoons baking soda
¼ teaspoon salt
½ teaspoon baking powder
1½ teaspoons cinnamon

¾ teaspoon nutmeg
2 cups coarsely grated
  unpeeled zucchini
1 can (about 20 ounces)
  crushed pineapple,
  preferably juice-packed,
  well drained
1 cup coarsely chopped
  walnuts

---

1. In a large bowl, beat the eggs. Gradually beat in the sugar until the mixture is thick and pale. Beat in the melted butter or margarine.
2. In another bowl, stir together the flours, baking soda, salt, baking powder, cinnamon, and nutmeg. Beat into the liquid mixture and then stir in the zucchini, pineapple, and walnuts.
3. Turn the batter into 2 greased and floured 9" x 5" loaf pans. Bake the breads in a 350° oven for 1 hour, or until they test done with a toothpick. Let pan cool on a rack before removing bread.

YIELD: 16 to 20 slices

CARROT–ZUCCHINI BREAD

Here's a healthful loaf that contains less than 1 cup of honey and jam for sweetening. The carrots and zucchini—two popular vegetables for breads—produce a chewy texture and attractive flavor. Like other breads of this type, this loaf stores well and makes for pleasant snacking almost any time of the day.

4 eggs
½ cup honey
6⅔ tablespoons butter or
  margarine, melted
1 cup yogurt
1 teaspoon vanilla
⅓ cup orange marmalade
1½ cups plus ⅓ cup whole
  wheat flour
1½ cups white flour

2 teaspoons baking powder
¾ teaspoon baking soda
2 teaspoons cinnamon
1 large carrot, grated
2 small zucchini (about 6"
  long), unpeeled and
  coarsely grated
½ cup coarsely chopped
  walnuts

1. In a large bowl, beat the eggs. Beat in the honey very well. Then beat in the melted butter, yogurt, vanilla, and orange marmalade.
2. In another bowl, stir together the flours, baking powder, baking soda, and cinnamon. Beat into the liquid mixture just until the dry ingredients are moistened. Stir in the carrot, zucchini, and walnuts.
3. Turn the batter into a greased and floured 9" x 5" loaf pan. Bake the bread in a 325° oven for 1½ hours, or until it tests done with a toothpick. Let pan cool on a rack before removing bread.

YIELD: 1 large loaf, or 10 to 12 slices

GRAHAM CRACKER BREAD

Crushed graham crackers make for a hearty, wholesome bread that's delicious spread with cream cheese for tea sandwiches. Use either packaged crumbs or crush crackers finely with a rolling pin or in a blender or food processor.

½ cup (1 stick) butter or
  margarine, softened
½ cup sugar
2 eggs
1 cup milk
¾ cup white flour
½ cup whole wheat flour
1⅔ cups graham cracker
  crumbs

1 tablespoon baking powder
¼ teaspoon salt
1 teaspoon cinnamon
½ cup raisins
½ cup coarsely chopped
  walnuts

---

1. In a bowl, cream the butter or margarine with the sugar. Beat in the eggs, then the milk.
2. In another bowl, stir together the flours, graham cracker crumbs, baking powder, salt, and cinnamon. Beat into the creamed mixture and then stir in the raisins and walnuts.
3. Turn the batter into a greased and floured 9" x 5" loaf pan. Bake the bread in a 350° oven for 1 hour, or until it tests done with a toothpick. Transfer pan to a rack to cool before removing bread.

YIELD: 8 to 10 slices

FRESH RHUBARB BREAD

Brown sugar sweetens the tart rhubarb in this extra-moist loaf that's lovely from the flecks of pink fruit. The bread makes a perfect springtime tea treat.

1 egg
1½ cups brown sugar
6 tablespoons (¾ stick) butter
   or margarine, melted
1 cup sour cream
2 tablespoons milk

1 teaspoon vanilla
1¼ cups white flour
1¼ cups whole wheat flour
1 teaspoon baking soda
¼ teaspoon salt
1½ cups diced raw rhubarb

1. In a bowl, gradually beat the brown sugar into the egg. Beat in the melted butter or margarine, then the sour cream, milk, and vanilla.
2. In another bowl, stir together the flours, baking soda, and salt. Beat into the liquid mixture and then stir in the rhubarb.
3. Turn the batter into a greased and floured 9" x 5" loaf pan. Bake the bread in a 325° oven for 1 hour and 10 minutes, or until it tests done with a toothpick. Transfer pan to a rack to cool before removing bread.

YIELD: 8 to 10 slices

APPLE–CARROT BREAD

Carrot bread has a new sweet twist in this loaf that's flecked with shredded apples. It's fine as a between-meal snack or as a lunch or brunch loaf.

4 tablespoons (½ stick) butter or margarine, softened
⅔ cups sugar
2 eggs
¾ cup white flour
1 cup whole wheat flour
1 teaspoon baking powder

1 teaspoon baking soda
¼ teaspoon salt
1½ cups peeled shredded apples
½ cup shredded carrot
½ cup coarsely chopped walnuts

---

1. In a bowl, cream the butter or margarine with the sugar. Beat in the eggs.
2. In another bowl, stir together the flours, baking powder, baking soda, and salt. Beat into the creamed mixture and then stir in the apples, carrot, and walnuts.
3. Turn the batter into a greased and floured 9" x 5" loaf pan. Bake the loaf in a 350° oven for 45 to 50 minutes, or until it tests done with a toothpick. Transfer pan to a rack to cool before removing bread.

YIELD: 8 to 10 slices

Nuts, Liqueurs, Jam, and Wine...
A Selection of Cakes with Other Wonderful Ingredients

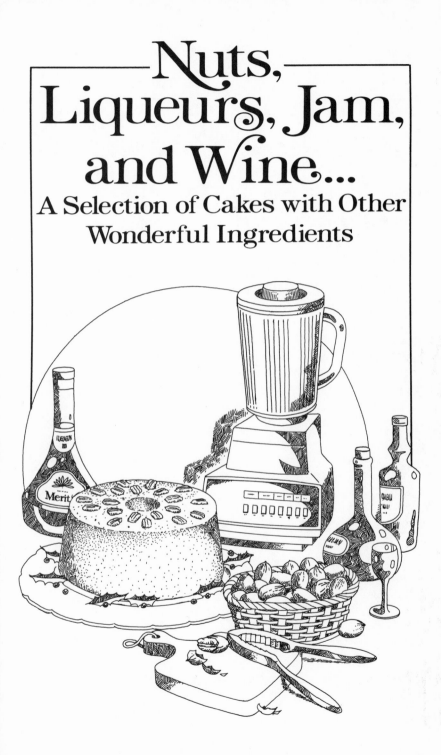

Into this chapter fall all the cakes that fit nowhere else, yet are far too delectable to be left out of the book entirely. Here you will find, among other treasured recipes, a chocolate- and almond-topped coffee cake, a rum-pecan cake from the South, a rich, rich nut cake flavored with raspberry jam, and a French fruitcake . . . in short, a delightful variety of thoroughly marvelous, all-occasion cakes.

You'll note that many of the cake recipes in this chapter are flavored primarily with nuts. Nuts are such a wonderful ingredient for cake-baking that you'll find them called for many times throughout the rest of the book as well.

Many of these recipes specify "ground" nuts. While some nuts may be purchased already ground, for the freshest flavor, it's best to grind them yourself. A food processor, equipped with the steel blade, does this job best. Most blenders cannot grind nuts adequately because they become too oily. If you don't have a food processor, you may chop the nuts very finely in an old-fashioned chopping bowl. You may also purchase inexpensive manual nut-grinders that work rather like pepper mills.

SOUTHERN RUM PECAN CAKE

Honey, rum, and pecans flavor this rich Southern loaf cake.

½ cup (1 stick) butter or
    margarine, softened
½ cup brown sugar
¼ cup honey
2 eggs
¼ cup water

½ cup dark rum
2 cups flour
2½ teaspoons baking powder
¼ teaspoon salt
1 cup coarsely chopped
    pecans

1. In a large bowl, cream the butter or margarine with the brown sugar and honey. Beat in the eggs, then the water and rum.

2. In another bowl, stir together the flour, baking powder, and salt. Beat into the creamed mixture. Stir in the pecans.
3. Turn the batter into a greased and floured 9" x 5" loaf pan. Bake the cake in a 375° oven for 45 to 50 minutes, or until it tests done with a toothpick. Let the cake cool on a rack.

YIELD: 8 to 10 slices

SWEDISH ALMOND CAKE

Although this is a cake, it's baked in a pie plate. Ground almonds line the plate, and there are plenty of nuts in the topping as well. Serve the cake in thin wedges, with dollop of whipped cream if you want to be fancy.

Cake Batter:

2 eggs	1 cup flour
¾ cup sugar	1½ teaspoons baking powder
½ cup (1 stick) butter, melted (use real butter, if possible)	⅛ teaspoon salt
	2 tablespoons ground blanched almonds
½ teaspoon almond extract	
¼ cup light cream or evaporated milk	

Topping: (Mix all ingredients in a saucepan and cook, stirring, until bubbly)

6 tablespoons (¾ stick) butter	¼ teaspoon nutmeg
	3 tablespoons honey
1 tablespoon flour	½ cup slivered, blanched almonds
2 teaspoons milk	

------

1. In a large bowl, beat the eggs. Gradually beat in the sugar until the mixture is thick and pale. Beat in the melted butter, then the almond extract and light cream.

2. In another bowl, stir together the flour, baking powder, and salt. Beat into the liquid mixture.
3. Butter a deep 9-inch pie plate and sprinkle it with the ground almonds. Spread the batter evenly in the plate. Bake the cake in a 325° oven for about 35 minutes, or until it is nearly done.
4. Turn the oven to 375°. Spread the topping evenly over the cake and bake about 10 minutes longer or until it is bubbly and slightly brown. Transfer the cake to a rack to cool.

YIELD: 10 servings

ALMOND BISCOTTI

These delightful Italian "cakes" are perfect with mid-morning tea or even for breakfast. Each long cake is sliced after partial baking and then baked again until browned on all edges. When cool, these become quite hard and so are marvelous when dunked into a hot beverage.

½ cup (1 stick) butter or
   margarine, softened
¾ cup sugar
3 eggs
2 tablespoons brandy
grated rind from 1 lemon
3 cups flour

2 teaspoons baking powder
¼ teaspoon salt
1 cup slivered almonds,
   toasted in an ungreased
   skillet until browned and
   then coarsely chopped

---

1. In a large bowl, cream the butter or margarine with the sugar. Beat in the eggs, then the brandy and lemon rind.
2. In another bowl, stir together the flour, baking powder, and salt. Beat into the creamed mixture along with the almonds. The batter will be very stiff.
3. With lightly floured hands, shape the mixture into two long cylinders on a greased baking sheet. Each should be about 15 inches long, 2½ inches wide, and ½ inch thick.

Bake the cylinders in a 350° oven for 20 minutes. They will not be fully baked.

4. Slice the cylinders on the diagonal into 1-inch slices. Place cut side down on the baking sheet and bake 20 to 25 minutes longer, or until very lightly browned.

YIELD: About 2 dozen biscotti

ALMOND RUM CAKE

Lemon juice and rind flavor this simple butter cake that has crunchy almonds all along the bottom crust and dark rum sprinkled over the baked cake. Although this cake is rather plain, it has a fine texture and is definitely worthy of any guests you may be having. To party it up, serve each slice with a scoop of the best vanilla ice cream.

3 eggs, separated
½ teaspoon cream of tartar
⅔ cup (10⅔ tablespoons) butter, softened (use real butter, if possible)
1½ cups sugar
1 teaspoon vanilla
1 teaspoon almond extract
2 tablespoons lemon juice

1 teaspoon grated lemon rind
¾ cup milk
2⅓ cups flour
2 teaspoons baking powder
¾ teaspoon baking soda
½ cup finely chopped blanched almonds
2 teaspoons dark rum

1. In a bowl, beat the egg whites with the cream of tartar until stiff. Set aside.
2. In a large bowl, cream the butter with the sugar (you need not clean the beaters between steps). Beat in the egg yolks, then the vanilla, almond extract, lemon juice and rind, and milk.
3. In another bowl, stir together the flour, baking powder, and baking soda. Beat into the creamed mixture. Stir in about

one-third of the egg whites to lighten the batter and then fold in the rest gently but thoroughly.

4. Grease well, but don't flour, a tube pan and sprinkle the almonds evenly on the bottom. Turn the batter into the pan. Bake the cake in a 300° oven for 1½ hours, or until it tests done with a toothpick. As soon as you remove it from the oven, sprinkle the top evenly with the rum. Transfer to a rack to cool.

YIELD: 14 servings

MARZIPAN CAKE

This is a most unusual version of pound cake. Chunks of marzipan mixed with ground almonds dot the batter, giving it a crunchy texture and very special flavor. Marzipan is a mixture of ground almonds and sugar and may be found in specialty food shops and many grocery stores.

Marzipan Mixture:
4½ ounces marzipan
1 cup ground almonds

1 tablespoon brandy

Cake Batter:
5 eggs, separated
pinch salt
1 cup (2 sticks) butter, softened (use real butter, if possible)

1 cup sugar
1 tablespoon brandy
1 teaspoon vanilla
2 cups flour

1. With a food processor or your hands, mix together the marzipan, almonds, and brandy until it holds together. On a surface dusted with confectioners' sugar, pat the mixture until it is about ½-inch thick. Cut it into ½-inch cubes.
2. In a bowl, beat the egg whites with the salt until stiff.
3. In a large bowl, cream the butter with the sugar. Beat in the egg yolks, then the brandy, vanilla, and flour.

4. Stir in about one-third of the beaten egg whites and then fold in the rest gently but thoroughly. Fold in the marzipan cubes.
5. Turn the batter into a greased and floured tube pan. Bake the cake in a 375° oven for about 65 minutes, or until it tests done with a toothpick. Transfer to a rack to cool.

YIELD: 12 servings

CRUNCH-TOPPED COFFEE CAKE

Almonds and semisweet chocolate top this orange-flavored coffee cake. It's delightful for brunch or as a snack between meals. The semisweet chocolate should be finely chopped; use either a blender or food processor—or else purchase miniature-size morsels.

⅔ cup (10⅔ tablespoons) butter or margarine, softened
1 cup sugar
2 eggs
1 tablespoon grated orange rind
⅔ cup orange juice

1 cup white flour
1 cup whole wheat flour
2½ teaspoons baking powder
¼ teaspoon salt
½ cup chopped almonds
½ cup finely chopped semisweet chocolate

1. In a large bowl, cream the butter or margarine with the sugar. Beat in the eggs, then the orange rind and juice.
2. In another bowl, stir together the flours, baking powder, and salt. Beat into the creamed mixture.
3. Turn the batter into a greased and floured 8" x 10" baking pan and sprinkle with the almonds and chocolate. Bake the cake in a 375° oven for 30 minutes, or until it tests done with a toothpick. Let cool on a rack. It is best to serve this cake directly from the pan; if you turn it out, the topping may fall off.

YIELD: 12 servings

PECAN SWIRL CAKE

A spicy pecan filling is layered through a rich sour cream cake that's well-flavored with coconut rum liqueur. The cake is ideal for brunch as a coffee cake or may also be served with a scoop of vanilla ice cream for a special family dessert.

Cake Batter:

½ cup (1 stick) butter or margarine, softened
1 cup granulated sugar
2 eggs
¾ cup sour cream
1 teaspoon vanilla

⅓ cup coconut rum liqueur
2 cups flour
¾ teaspoon baking soda
1 teaspoon baking powder
½ teaspoon nutmeg
¼ teaspoon salt

Nut Filling: (Mix together all ingredients)

⅓ cup coarsely chopped pecans
⅓ cup brown sugar

¼ teaspoon cinnamon
¼ teaspoon nutmeg

1. In a bowl, cream the butter or margarine with the sugar. Beat in the eggs, then the sour cream, vanilla, and liqueur.
2. In another bowl, stir together the flour, baking soda, baking powder, nutmeg, and salt. Beat into the creamed mixture.
3. Turn one-third of the batter into a greased and floured tube pan. Sprinkle with half the filling. Repeat the layers, and end with the final third of the batter, spreading it evenly.
4. Bake the cake in a 350° oven for 55 to 60 minutes, or until it tests done with a toothpick. Let cool on a rack.

YIELD: 10 to 12 servings

RASPBERRY NUT BUTTER CAKE

Here's a cake rich enough to show off at your fanciest dinner party. The raspberry jam gives the cake a lively pink color. A sprinkling of confectioners' sugar over the top just before serving will enhance the attractiveness of this remarkably delectable tube cake.

6 eggs, separated
1 cup (2 sticks) butter,
    softened (use real butter,
    if possible)
1½ cups sugar
¾ cup seedless raspberry,
    black raspberry, or
    blackberry jam

1 tablespoon vanilla
¼ cup dark rum
1 cup minus 1 tablespoon
    flour
1 teaspoon baking powder
¾ cup ground walnuts
¾ cup ground pecans

----

1. In a bowl, beat the egg whites until stiff. Set aside.
2. In a large bowl, beat the butter with the sugar until thoroughly creamed. Beat in the egg yolks, then the jam, vanilla, and rum.
3. In a small bowl, stir together the flour and baking powder. Beat into the creamed mixture, then stir in the nuts. Stir about one-third of the egg whites into the batter to lighten it and then fold in the rest gently but thoroughly.
4. Turn the batter into a greased and floured tube pan. Bake the cake in a 350° oven for 65 to 70 minutes, or until it tests done with a toothpick. Transfer to a rack to cool.

YIELD: 12 servings

AUSTRIAN NUT CAKE

This cake, containing sour cream, lots of butter, and two cups of walnuts, is ultrarich—and ultraspecial. Serve it to guests when you want to make an impressive yet quick and easy dessert.

1 cup (2 sticks) butter, softened (use real butter, if possible)	2 tablespoons dark rum
	2⅔ cups flour
	4 teaspoons baking powder
2 cups brown sugar	1 teaspoon cinnamon
3 eggs	1 teaspoon nutmeg
1 cup sour cream	2 cups ground walnuts

1. In a large bowl, cream the butter with the brown sugar. Beat in the eggs, then the sour cream and rum.
2. In another bowl, stir together the flour, baking powder, and spices. Beat into the creamed mixture and then stir in the walnuts.
3. Turn the batter into a greased and floured tube pan. Bake the cake in a 350° oven for 1 hour and 20 minutes, or until it tests done with a toothpick. Transfer to a rack to cool.

YIELD: 14 to 16 servings

TYROLEAN NUT CAKE

This attractive "cake" is actually made up of 1-inch balls that are baked side-by-side. Although the balls start out almost like cookies, when baked they form a single layer. To eat, use a sharp knife to cut between the edges of each original ball. These little morsels are buttery-rich and filled with crunchy walnuts. They make a delicious snack when accompanied by a cup of tea.

½ cup (1 stick) butter, softened (use real butter, if possible)
¾ cup plus 1 tablespoon sugar
2 eggs
1 teaspoon vanilla

1 teaspoon almond extract
2½ cups flour
2 teaspoons baking powder
¼ teaspoon salt
1½ cups finely chopped walnuts

1. In a bowl, cream the butter with ¾ cup sugar. Beat in the eggs and extracts.
2. In another bowl, stir together the flour, baking powder, and salt. Beat into the creamed mixture until incorporated and then beat in the walnuts. The batter will be stiff.
3. Roll small pieces of the batter into 1-inch balls and place, touching, in a greased and floured 9-inch layer cake pan. (If you make concentric circles, the balls should just fill the pan.) Sprinkle with the remaining 1 tablespoon sugar.
4. Bake the cake in a 350° oven for about 50 minutes, or until golden brown. Let cool on a rack.

YIELD: About 3 dozen balls

HAZELNUT CAKE

Hazelnuts are rich and costly but well worth the price, since their special flavor cannot be matched by any other nut. This densely textured cake is somewhat like a pound cake, and the layer of nuts on the bottom gives the crust a delicious crunchiness.

1 cup (2 sticks) butter, softened (use real butter, if possible)
1¾ cups sugar
3 whole eggs plus 1 egg yolk
¾ cup milk

1 tablespoon vanilla
2¾ cups flour
½ teaspoon salt
2¼ teaspoons baking powder
1 cup finely chopped hazelnuts

---

1. In a large bowl, cream the butter with the sugar. Beat in the eggs and egg yolk, then the milk and vanilla.
2. In another bowl, stir together the flour, salt, and baking powder. Beat into the creamed mixture.
3. Grease well but do not flour a tube pan and sprinkle the hazelnuts evenly over the bottom. Turn the batter into the pan. Bake the cake in a 350° oven for 65 minutes, or until it tests done with a toothpick. Let cool on a rack. Serve the cake upside down, so the nuts are on top.

YIELD: 16 servings

HONEY SUNFLOWER CAKE

Sunflower seeds and sunflower seed meal (made by grinding unsalted sunflower seeds in a blender or food processor until they are nearly as fine as flour) impart a rich nutlike flavor to this honey spice cake. Honey in baked goods usually makes for excellent keeping qualities—and this cake is no exception.

½ cup (1 stick) butter or
  margarine, softened
1 cup honey
2 eggs
1 teaspoon vanilla
1 cup strong coffee
2 cups whole wheat flour
½ cup wheat germ
¼ cup nonfat dry milk
  powder

½ cup sunflower seed meal
¼ teaspoon cinnamon
¼ teaspoon nutmeg
1 teaspoon baking soda
¼ teaspoon salt
¾ cup unsalted sunflower
  seeds
½ cup dark raisins
½ cup golden raisins

1. In a bowl, cream the butter or margarine with the honey. Beat in the eggs, then the vanilla and coffee.
2. In another bowl, stir together the flour, wheat germ, milk powder, sunflower seed meal, spices, baking soda, and salt. Beat into the creamed mixture and then stir in the sunflower seeds and raisins.
3. Turn the batter into a greased and floured 9" x 13" baking pan. Bake the cake in a 350° oven for 30 minutes, or until it tests clean with a toothpick. Transfer to a rack to cool.

YIELD: 16 servings

ONE-TWO-THREE-FOUR CAKE, WITH VARIATIONS

The name of this cake doesn't refer to the speed at which it's put together. Rather, the recipe is an old-fashioned one that originally called for 1 cup of butter, 2 cups of sugar, 3 cups of flour, and 4 eggs. Actually, the recipe has stood the test of time remarkably well and this one just calls for a little less flour in the interest of lightness. Although this is a "plain" cake, the separately beaten egg whites give it a wonderful texture and the simple ingredients make for a most appealing flavor. The cake lends itself to several delightful variations, two of which are given below.

4 eggs, separated
1 cup (2 sticks) butter,
   softened (use real butter,
   if possible)
2 cups sugar
1½ teaspoons vanilla

1 cup milk
2½ cups plus 1 tablespoon
   flour
2¼ teaspoons baking powder
¼ teaspoon salt

1. In a bowl, beat the egg whites until stiff. Set aside.
2. In a large bowl, cream the butter with the sugar. Beat in the egg yolks, then the vanilla and milk.
3. In another bowl, stir together the flour, baking powder, and salt. Beat into the creamed mixture. Stir in one-third of the egg whites and then fold in the rest gently but thoroughly.
4. Turn the batter into a greased and floured tube pan. Bake in a 350° oven for about 1 hour, or until the cake tests done with a toothpick. Transfer to a rack to cool.

YIELD: 16 servings

Lemon Cream Cheese Cake: Substitute 1 8-ounce package softened cream cheese for the butter. Add the grated rind of 1 lemon along with the vanilla and milk.

Coconut Cake: After you have stirred in one-third of the beaten egg whites, stir in ¾ cup shredded sweetened coconut.

SPONGE CAKE

A sponge cake is a remarkably versatile recipe to have in your files, particularly during the summer months. It's light enough to enjoy on the hottest of days and goes well with a scoop of ice cream or a topping of whipped cream and blueberries or freshly sliced peaches.

6 eggs, separated
½ teaspoon cream of tartar
pinch salt
¾ cup sugar

1 tablespoon fresh lemon
  juice
1 cup flour

1. In a bowl, beat the egg whites with the cream of tartar and salt. Set aside.
2. In another bowl, beat the egg yolks. Gradually beat in the sugar until the mixture is thick and pale. Beat in the lemon juice, then the flour. Stir in one-third of the egg whites and then fold in the rest gently but thoroughly.
3. Turn the batter into a greased and floured tube pan. Bake the cake in a 350° oven for about 40 minutes, or until it tests done with a toothpick. Transfer to a rack to cool.

YIELD: 8 to 10 servings

MARMORKUCHEN (GERMAN MARBLE CAKE)

This is a lovely-textured, almond and chocolate marble cake. It slices beautifully—almost like a pound cake—and is wonderful with a scoop of vanilla ice cream.

1 cup (2 sticks) butter (use
  real butter, if possible)
1½ cups sugar
4 eggs
1 cup milk
1 teaspoon almond extract

3¼ cups flour
1 tablespoon baking powder
⅛ teaspoon salt
¼ cup cocoa, sifted if lumpy
3 tablespoons dark rum

1. In a large bowl, cream the butter with the sugar. Beat in the eggs, then the milk and almond extract.
2. In another bowl, stir together the flour, baking powder, and salt. Beat into the creamed mixture.
3. Turn half the batter into another bowl and stir in the cocoa and rum.
4. Grease a tube pan and flour it. Layer the light and dark batters by large spoonfuls and then swirl slightly with a knife.
5. Bake the cake in a 350° oven for about 70 minutes, or until it tests done with a toothpick. Transfer to a rack to cool.

YIELD: 14 to 16 servings

GRAHAM SOUR CREAM CAKE

Crushed graham crackers add a homey touch to this rich sour cream tube cake that's dotted with raisins and crunchy almonds.

2 cups graham cracker crumbs
1 cup sour cream
½ cup (1 stick) butter or margarine, softened
1 cup brown sugar
2 eggs
1 cup milk
2 teaspoons grated orange rind

2 teaspoons vanilla
2 cups minus 2 tablespoons flour
1 teaspoon baking powder
1 teaspoon baking soda
¼ teaspoon salt
1 cup slivered blanched almonds
1 cup raisins

1. In a small bowl, stir together the graham cracker crumbs and sour cream and let sit until they are needed.
2. In a large bowl, cream the butter or margarine with the brown sugar. Beat in the eggs, then the milk, orange rind, vanilla, and graham mixture.

3. In another bowl, stir together the flour, baking powder, baking soda, and salt. Beat into the creamed mixture. Stir in the almonds and raisins.
4. Turn the batter into a greased and floured tube pan. Bake the cake in a 350° oven for 1 hour, or until it tests done. Let cool on a rack.

YIELD: 14 to 16 servings

BLACK FOREST COFFEE CAKE

From Germany comes this wonderfully rich and hearty coffee cake that's strewn with raisins, pecans, and spices. For a fancy brunch, it can't be beat.

Cake Batter:

¾ cup (1½ sticks) butter, softened (use real butter, if possible)
1½ cups granulated sugar
3 eggs
2 teaspoons vanilla

2 cups sour cream
3 cups flour
1½ teaspoons baking powder
1½ teaspoons baking soda
¼ teaspoon salt

Filling: (Mix all ingredients together well)

¾ cup brown sugar
1½ tablespoons cinnamon
1½ tablespoons cocoa, sifted if lumpy

¾ cup raisins
¾ cup chopped pecans

---

1. In a large bowl, cream the butter with the sugar. Beat in the eggs, then the vanilla and sour cream.
2. In another bowl, stir together the flour, baking powder, baking soda, and salt. Beat into the creamed ingredients just until moistened.
3. In a large tube pan that has been greased and floured, make layers of batter and filling so that you begin and end

with batter and have five layers of batter and four layers of filling in between.

4. Bake the cake in a 350° oven for 1½ hours, or until it tests done with a toothpick. Let cool on a rack.

YIELD: 16 servings

STOLLEN

Stollen is a German coffee cake that's made for Christmas and contains a plentitude of nuts and fruits. Most versions of stollen are made with a yeasted dough, but this quick recipe takes far less time. The addition of farmer's cheese to the dough gives it a fresh, dairy-like flavor.

¾ cup (1½ sticks) butter, softened (use real butter, if possible)
1⅛ cups sugar
3 eggs
8 ounces farmer's cheese (or substitute very dry cottage cheese)
1 tablespoon dark rum
¼ teaspoon vanilla
¼ teaspoon almond extract

4 cups flour
1¼ teaspoons baking powder
⅛ teaspoon cardamon
⅛ teaspoon nutmeg
1 cup ground walnuts
⅞ cup ground almonds
1 cup dark raisins
1 cup golden raisins
½ cup chopped candied orange peel

---

1. In a very large bowl, cream the butter with the sugar. Beat in the eggs, then the farmer's cheese, rum, and extracts.
2. In another bowl, stir together the flour, baking powder, cardamon, and nutmeg. Beat into the creamed mixture. The batter will be very stiff. Stir in the nuts, raisins, and orange peel. It may be necessary to use your hands for this.
3. Form the batter into a large oval on a greased and floured 11" x 16" baking sheet. Bake the stollen in a 350° oven for

about 1 hour and 25 minutes, or until the cake is lightly browned and tests done with a toothpick. Transfer to a rack to cool. Before serving, dust with confectioners' sugar, if desired. To serve, cut into thin slices.

YIELD: About 30 servings

BRAN STREUSEL CAKE

This honey-flavored cake is hearty from the addition of bran and whole wheat flour. A dried-fruit streusel mixture is layered through the batter, making the sliced cake particularly attractive.

Cake Batter:
¾ cup (1½ sticks) butter or margarine, softened
¾ cup granulated sugar
¾ cup honey
2 eggs
1 tablespoon grated orange rind
½ teaspoon almond extract
1 cup milk
1¼ cups white flour
1 cup whole wheat flour
1 cup bran cereal, such as All-Bran
2½ teaspoons baking powder

Streusel Filling: (Mix all ingredients together until crumbly)
4 tablespoons (½ stick) butter or margarine, melted
½ cup brown sugar
1½ teaspoons cinnamon
½ cup bran cereal
¼ cup raisins
¼ cup finely diced dried pears (if unavailable, substitute dried apples)
¼ cup finely diced dried apricots

---

1. In a large bowl, cream together the butter or margarine with the sugar and honey. Beat in the eggs, then the orange rind, almond extract, and milk.

2. In another bowl, stir together the flours, bran cereal, and baking powder. Beat into the creamed mixture.
3. Grease and flour a tube pan and pour in ⅓ of the batter. Cover with half the streusel mixture. Then pour on another third of the batter. Cover with the rest of the streusel mixture and then the remaining batter.
4. Bake the cake in a 350° oven for 1¼ hours, or until it tests done with a toothpick. Let cool on a rack.

YIELD: 16 servings

GRAPE NUT CAKE

Grape Nuts cereal adds a pleasantly chewy texture and wholesome flavor to this cake. The combination of pecans, brown sugar, and coconut makes the batter taste remarkably like the delicious filling of a classic German chocolate cake. It's delicious served warm from the oven.

1 cup Grape Nuts cereal
1 cup boiling water
½ cup (1 stick) butter or margarine, softened
¾ cup brown sugar
¾ cup granulated sugar
2 eggs
1 teaspoon vanilla

1 cup white flour
½ cup whole wheat flour
¼ teaspoon salt
¾ teaspoon baking powder
½ cup coarsely chopped pecans
¼ cup shredded coconut

1. Pour the boiling water over the Grape Nuts and let sit until ready to use in the batter.
2. In a large bowl, cream the butter or margarine with the sugars. Beat in the eggs, then the vanilla and Grape Nuts, along with any water that was not absorbed.

3. In another bowl, stir together the flours, salt, and baking powder. Beat into the Grape Nuts mixture. Stir in the pecans and coconut.
4. Turn the batter into a greased and floured 9" x 13" baking pan. Bake the cake in a 350° oven for 30 minutes, or until it tests done with a toothpick. Let cool on a rack.

YIELD: 12 servings

VERMONT WINE LOAF

Maple syrup and wine make for a moist loaf cake that's a nice addition to a fruit dessert and also packs well for the lunch box.

½ cup (1 stick) butter or margarine, softened
½ cup brown sugar
1 egg
¼ cup maple syrup
¼ cup dry red wine

1¼ cups flour
1 teaspoon baking powder
¼ teaspoon baking soda
¼ teaspoon salt
½ teaspoon nutmeg
½ cup chopped walnuts

1. In a bowl, cream the butter or margarine with the brown sugar. Beat in the egg, then the maple syrup and wine.
2. In another bowl, stir together the flour, baking powder, baking soda, salt, and nutmeg. Beat into the maple mixture and then stir in the walnuts.
3. Turn the batter into a greased and floured 9" x 5" loaf pan. Bake the cake in a 350° oven for 40 minutes, or until it tests done with a toothpick. Transfer to a rack to cool.

YIELD: 8 slices

MINCEMEAT UPSIDE-DOWN CAKE

Without doubt, this should be the dessert at your next Christmas dinner. Rich mincemeat, enhanced with rum and pecans, forms the topping for this impressive and festive cake. Serve it warm from the oven or at room temperature, plain or with a scoop of ice cream or a dollop of hard sauce.

Cake Batter:

¾ cup (1½ sticks) butter or margarine, softened
1½ cups granulated sugar
3 eggs
1½ teaspoons vanilla
1½ cups milk
1½ cups white flour

1½ cups whole wheat flour
¼ teaspoon salt
1 teaspoon cinnamon
½ teaspoon nutmeg
1 tablespoon baking powder

Topping:

4 tablespoons (½ stick) butter or margarine
½ cup brown sugar
1 cup coarsely chopped pecans

1 1½-pound jar mincemeat (about 3 cups)
⅓ cup dark rum

---

1. In a bowl, cream the butter or margarine with the granulated sugar. Beat in the eggs, then the vanilla and milk.
2. In another bowl, stir together the flours, salt, spices, and baking powder. Beat into the creamed mixture.
3. As the oven is preheating to 350°, place the butter or margarine for the topping in a 9" x 13" baking pan and let it melt in the oven. Remove the pan from the oven and tilt so the butter coats all surfaces. Stir in the brown sugar and spread the mixture evenly over the bottom of the pan. Sprinkle with the pecans. Stir together the mincemeat and rum and spread over the pecans. Gently pour in the batter.

4. Bake the cake in the 350° oven for 55 minutes. Run a knife around the edge and then turn the cake upside down onto a baking sheet. Bake the cake 10 minutes longer. Transfer to a rack to cool.

YIELD: 24 servings

PIÑA COLADA CAKE

Here's an upside-down cake with all the flavors of the popular piña colada cocktail—pineapple, rum, and coconut.

Pineapple Layer:

1 20-oz. crushed pineapple, juice-packed (drain and reserve ½ cup syrup)

¼ cup (½ stick) butter or margarine, melted

¼ cup dark rum

¼ cup canned cream of coconut

Cake Batter:

½ cup (1 stick) butter or margarine, softened

1¼ cups sugar

2 eggs

¾ cup canned cream of coconut

¼ cup reserved pineapple syrup

2⅔ cups flour

¼ teaspoon salt

2½ teaspoons baking powder

1. Stir together all ingredients in the pineapple layer plus ¼ cup of the reserved syrup from the can. Spread evenly in the bottom of a greased 9" x 13" baking pan.
2. In a large bowl, cream the butter or margarine with the sugar. Beat in the eggs, then the cream of coconut and pineapple syrup.

3. In another bowl, stir together the flour, salt, and baking powder. Beat into the creamed mixture.

4. Turn the batter into the prepared pan. Bake the cake in a 350° oven for 1 hour, or until it tests done with a toothpick. Run a knife around the edges and tip out onto a large platter or baking sheet. Let cool on a rack. NOTE: Because this cake is so moist, any leftovers should be stored in the refrigerator.

YIELD: 20 servings

FRENCH FRUITCAKE

This type of fruitcake in France is traditionally served at birthday celebrations. The cake is similar to our Christmas fruitcakes, except the foreign version contains far more batter in proportion to fruit. Also, there's no waiting period before enjoying the cake (most American fruitcakes, as you probably are aware, are aged before slicing).

¾ cup chopped candied
  orange peel
½ cup coarsely chopped
  walnuts
½ cup dark raisins
½ cup golden raisins
1½ cups plus 2 tablespoons
  flour, divided usage
½ cup (1 stick) butter or
  margarine, softened

½ cup sugar
2½ tablespoons honey
2 eggs
1½ tablespoons light cream
  or evaporated milk
2 tablespoons dark rum
1 teaspoon vanilla
½ teaspoon baking powder

1. Toss the candied orange peel, walnuts, and raisins with 2 tablespoons flour, and set aside.

2. In a large bowl, cream the butter or margarine with the sugar and honey. Beat in the egg , then the cream or milk, rum, and vanilla.
3. In another bowl, stir together the remaining 1½ cups flour and the baking powder. Beat into the creamed mixture and then stir in the fruits and nuts.
4. Turn the batter into a greased and floured 9" x 5" loaf pan. Bake the cake in a 350° oven for 10 minutes. Lower the heat to 325° and bake the cake 45 minutes longer, or until it tests done with a toothpick. Transfer to a rack to cool.

YIELD: 8 to 10 slices

COGNAC FRENCH CAKES

This recipe yields two cakes, each looking like a huge cookie. The recipe comes from the Cognac region of France, where the cakes, thinly sliced into long strips, are served with fruit and Cognac after dinner. They also make a delightful between-meal snack with a cup of tea.

10 tablespoons (1 stick plus 2 tablespoons) butter, softened (use real butter, if possible)
¾ cup sugar
3 eggs (reserve 1 yolk for glaze)
3 tablespoons brandy

2 teaspoons grated orange rind
3 cups flour
2 teaspoons baking powder
⅛ teaspoon salt
½ cup raisins, halved

1. In a bowl, cream the butter with the sugar. Beat in the eggs, then the brandy and orange rind.
2. In another bowl, stir together the flour, baking powder, and salt. Beat into the creamed mixture and then stir in the raisins.

3. Divide the dough in half and, using lightly floured hands, pat each into an eight-inch circle on a greased baking sheet. Mix the reserved egg yolk with 1 teaspoon water. Brush on the cakes. Using the tines of a fork, make a criss-cross pattern all across the top of each cake.
4. Bake the cakes in a 375° oven for 20 to 25 minutes, or until a rich golden brown. Let cool thoroughly and then wrap in plastic. NOTE: These are best if left to age overnight before eating. Kept wrapped in plastic, they stay fresh at room temperature for about 1 week. They also freeze well.

YIELD: 2 cakes, each serving 6 to 8

LEMON-FILLED MACAROON

This cake is like a big cookie that's filled with a chewy lemon-almond mixture. It has a simple homeyness that makes it especially appealing. Well wrapped, it keeps fresh for several days.

Cake Batter:

1 cup (2 sticks) butter or margarine, softened
1 cup sugar
1 egg

1 teaspoon vanilla
1⅓ cups white flour
1⅓ cups whole wheat flour
⅛ teaspoon salt

Filling: (Mix all ingredients together well)

1 cup finely chopped almonds
1 tablespoon grated lemon rind

1 egg, beaten slightly
½ cup sugar

1. In a bowl, cream the butter or margarine with the sugar. Beat in the egg, then the vanilla.

2. In another bowl, stir together the flours and salt. Beat into the creamed mixture. The batter will be stiff (like a cookie batter).

3. Spread about one-third of the batter into the bottom of a greased 9-inch round cake pan. Pat down with your fingertips to make even. Spread with the filling. Cover with the remaining batter. (The easiest way to do this is to pat tablespoons of dough between your palms and drop all over the top of the cake. Then pinch these pieces together to connect. Don't worry if the top isn't completely even.)

4. Bake the cake in a 325° oven for about 1 hour, or until it is browned and tests done with a toothpick. Let cool on a rack. Cut into wedges to serve.

YIELD: 12 to 14 servings

A Selection Of Basic Icings...

For Those Who Won't Eat Cake Without Them

The cakes in this book are so flavorful in themselves, there is no need to frost them. However, there are people who claim to actually prefer the icing to the cake. And to these people, no matter how delicious, a cake cannot be complete unless it's adorned with a rich, creamy coating.

Icings and frostings do have the advantage of protecting the cake from drying out. And they also make for a more festive appearance, which is a bonus if you're planning to serve the cake to guests.

Although I rarely ice my cakes, there are times when I do crave that extra sweetness. And so, over the years I've developed a few favorite icings, frostings, and glazes. This chapter includes several that are quickly prepared and fool-proof.

There are basically three types of frostings—glazes, icings, and true frostings. A glaze is quite thin and usually dribbled over the cake. The top of the cake is covered, with just enough glaze running down the sides to look appealing. It's especially good on the cakes in this book because it adds a hint of sweetness without overwhelming the cake.

Icings are a cross between glazes and frostings, being thicker than a glaze but still without the body of a frosting. Icings cover the cake completely and are attractively shiny.

Finally, frostings are for the true lover of iced cakes. Thick and creamy, the frosting is applied liberally and adds a sweet, rich quality that the unfrosted cake can never achieve.

It should be noted that the cake must be thoroughly cooled before any type of icing or frosting is applied. Otherwise the frosting will seal the cake, trapping the steam inside and making it soggy. Also, a warm cake will melt the frosting, making a mess.

CONFECTIONERS' GLAZE

This is one of the simplest of all icings. Just sift confectioners' sugar into a bowl and add enough milk or freshly squeezed lemon juice to make a thin glaze. Either dribble it over your cake or spread it with a knife. Let extra glaze build up around the edges of the cake, so the glaze runs down the sides. Made with milk, this is especially nice on chocolate tube cakes, since the icing lends an attractive look and extra sweetness without appreciably affecting the chocolate flavor. For spiced tube cakes, make the glaze with lemon juice.

APRICOT OR CURRANT GLAZE

These glazes, quickly made from jam or jelly, add an appealing color and flavor to the finished cake. They are particularly good on fruit, vegetable, and spice cakes. NOTE: These two flavors are especially common in French baking as glazes for cakes and tarts. But other favorite jam or jelly flavors can also be used. One that I enjoy is strawberry. If you use other jams (or preserves or marmalades), they must be pressed through a sieve. Jellies are smooth enough, so this step is not required.

½ cup apricot preserves,   2 tablespoons sugar
   pressed through a sieve or
   ½ cup currant jelly

Heat the sieved preserves or unsieved jelly with the sugar in a small saucepan, stirring, until it is hot and thin. Either dribble the glaze over the cake or spread it with a knife. Let extra glaze build up around the edges of the cake, so it runs down the sides.

YIELD: ½ cup glaze

CHOCOLATE GLAZE

This glaze is attractively smooth and shiny. It's extremely easy to make and perks up an orange or marble tube cake.

2½ tablespoons butter or
  margarine, melted
3 tablespoons cocoa, sifted
  if lumpy

½ cup confectioners' sugar
½ teaspoon vanilla
about 1 tablespoon hot water

In a bowl, beat together the melted butter, cocoa, sugar, and vanilla. Beat in the water gradually until the mixture is thin and of a good consistency. Drizzle over cake immediately.
YIELD: About ½ cup, or enough to barely cover a tube cake (for a thicker coating, double all ingredients)

LEMON ICING

This is my mother's recipe and I have been making it for years. It's especially good on hearty cakes, such as an apple-sauce or carrot loaf. The recipe makes enough for two loaf cakes but may be stored in the refrigerator and reheated. It may also be used on a tube or rectangular cake.

1 cup granulated sugar
⅓ cup milk
2 tablespoons butter

¼ teaspoon salt
1 teaspoon grated lemon rind

---

1. Place the sugar, milk, butter, and salt in a small saucepan. Bring to a rolling boil and boil, stirring, for 1 minute. Remove from the heat and stir in the lemon rind.
2. Let stand until cooled and slightly thickened. Drizzle over the top and sides of the cake.
YIELD: About 1 cup icing

WHITE BUTTER ICING

This is my least favorite frosting, but I am including it for those who prefer to ice a chocolate cake with vanilla frosting or who tint white icings for birthday and other celebratory cakes. As in Chocolate Butter Frosting, it is difficult to give exact measurements. After you have added the confectioners' sugar, add enough milk to give the icing a good consistency for spreading. You may also wish to add a bit more vanilla for a stronger flavor. For additional color and flavor, you may stir into the icing ½ cup finely chopped raisins, shredded coconut, toasted blanched almonds, or chopped cherries (either candied or maraschino).

3 tablespoons butter, softened   about ¼ cup milk
2 teaspoons vanilla
about 2 cups confectioners'
sugar

Cream the butter, vanilla, confectioners' sugar, and about half the milk. Add additional milk until the frosting is of a good consistency for spreading.

YIELD: About 1¼ cups, or enough for a 9" x 13" or tube cake.

CHOCOLATE BUTTER FROSTING

This must be the world's most popular frosting, as it's easy to prepare, makes a chocolate cake even more fudgy, and adds extra color and flavor to a white or marble cake. It's hard to give exact proportions in this recipe. Just add enough confectioners' sugar so that it is sweet enough for your tastes (I like it on the bittersweet side) and then enough milk so that it will spread easily.

2 ounces unsweetened
   chocolate
3 tablespoons butter
1 teaspoon vanilla

about ¼ cup milk
about 2 cups sifted
   confectioners' sugar

In a medium-sized saucepan, melt the chocolate with the butter. Remove from the heat and stir in the vanilla and about half the milk. Beat in confectioners' sugar until it's sweet enough for your tastes and then beat in just enough milk to make the frosting a good consistency for spreading.

YIELD: About 1½ cups, or enough for a 9" x 13" or a tube cake

RICH CHOCOLATE FROSTING

Plenty of chocolate and heavy cream make this the ultimate in chocolate frostings. It's heavy and fudgelike, great for covering a devil's food cake.

¾ cup sugar   5 tablespoons butter
⅔ cup heavy cream   ½ teaspoon vanilla
3 squares unsweetened
  chocolate

1. Place the sugar and cream in a small heavy saucepan. Bring to a boil, stirring. Reduce heat so mixture is barely boiling and let cook, undisturbed, 6 minutes. Remove from heat and add chocolate and butter. Stir until melted and then stir in the vanilla.
2. Beat mixture until cooled, thick, and creamy.

YIELD: About 1 cup, or enough for a 9" x 13" or tube cake

HONEYED ORANGE FROSTING

This cooked frosting takes a little more time than uncooked icings, but the result is worth it. The frosting is thick and light, and swirls in grand peaks. The color is pale, with just a hint of gold. The orange flavor complements many cakes, particularly chocolate and vanilla ones.

1¼ cups granulated sugar
¼ cup honey
¼ teaspoon cream of tartar
⅓ cup orange juice

1 tablespoon lemon juice
2 egg whites
⅛ teaspoon salt

---

1. Place all ingredients in the top of a double boiler and cook over rapidly boiling water, beating constantly with an electric mixer, for exactly 7 minutes.
2. Remove from the heat and continue beating until thickened and a good consistency for spreading.

YIELD: About 2½ cups, or enough for the top and sides of a 9-inch layer cake or a 9" x 13" rectangular cake. Unless you like your frosting very thick, this will probably yield a little more than you would need for a tube cake.

Index